The
COLLEGE
GUIDE for
PARENTS

The COLLEGE GUIDE for PARENTS

Charles J. Shields

College Entrance Examination Board
New York

Copies of this book may be ordered from College Board Publications, Box 886, New York, New York 10101-0886. The price is $12.95.

Editorial inquiries concerning this book should be directed to Editorial Office, The College Board, 45 Columbus Avenue, New York, New York, 10023-6992.

First edition published by Surrey Books.

Cover design by Terrence Fehr.

Library of Congress Catalog Number: 88-070580
ISBN: 0-87447-316-0

Printed in the United States of America

9 8 7 6 5 4 3 2 1

Contents

1 **Is Your Child College Bound for the "Right" Reasons?** A self-appraisal for your child showing whether college is in the picture. Reasons that young people go to college. Alternatives to college. Goal-clarification exercise. Tips on how much you should get involved in your teenager's planning. ▶ *page 3*

2 **Starting the Countdown to College** A College Information Checklist of things your child needs to know about preparing for college. A step-by-step calendar to help keep track of important deadlines leading up to college. ▶ *page 14*

3 **The Importance of Your Child's High School Coursework** How to get the most out of working with your child's counselor. A counselor-parent checklist. Which high school courses your child should take for college. How to cope with academic problems. Zeroing in on the best of what your child's high school has to offer. How to polish up a high school record. ▶ *page 21*

4 **How to Make the Right College Choice** Comparing colleges in terms of location, admissions selectivity, size, social activities, cost, and programs. Using a college handbook. How to get key information from a college's own catalog. Helping your child narrow down choices. Visiting a college campus. Your child's chances of getting into the college of his or her first choice. How to avoid pushing your child into the wrong school. ▶ *page 36*

Acknowledgments

I'm indebted to the following people for their contributions to this book:

Philip N. Chor, M.D., Rush-Presbyterian St. Luke's Hospital, Chicago; Jim Alexander, College Consultant, Highland Park High School, Highland Park, Illinois; the late Dan Hall; Dave Simpson, computer consultant and long-time friend; the staff of the Midwest Regional Office of the College Board, Evanston, Illinois, and especially A. Steven Graff, Director for Admissions and Guidance Services for the Board's Midwest Office; the staff of the National Association of College Admission Counselors, Skokie, Illinois; the administration of Homewood-Flossmoor High School, Flossmoor, Illinois, especially Eleanor Steiner, librarian, and my colleagues in the guidance department; Beth Pollock and Harriet Gershman, Educational Consultants, Academic Counseling Services, Inc., Munster, Indiana; Ellen Parker, editor of *Key Magazine;* Mary Beauchamp, Associate Director of Admissions, and Daniel C. Walls, Director of Admissions, Emory University; Zina Jacques, Director of Admissions, Mills College; Antony Moriarty, Director of Pupil and Pesonnel Services, Rich East Township High School, Park Forest, Illinois; Douglas Gertner, former Assistant Director of Admissions, Kenyon College; Harold Wingood, Assistant Director of Admissions, Tufts University; Wilma Wallace, Assistant Director of Admissions, Brown University; Don Hancock, Assistant Director of Admissions, Yale University; Marti Clark, former Director of Admissions, Illinois College; Michael Steinberg, Brisk, Rubin & Steinberg Literary Agency, Evanston, Illinois; Ted O'Neill, Associate Director of Admissions, the University of Chicago, who introduced me to Susan H. Schwartz, publisher of Surrey Books; my father, Charles J. Shields, who gave generously of his advice and encouragement while teaching me to write; and Carolyn Trager, my editor at the College Board, who cheerfully accepts the hard work of guiding authors and bringing forth their books.

Foreword

You want your child to select the best college. Define *best*. Does *best* mean that your child decides to attend your alma mater? Does it mean the number one school on the latest list of the 10 *best* colleges?

Second question: What role should you play in the selection process? How involved should you be? I remember the father who bluntly stated to me, "My son has complete responsibility for picking his college. I want nothing to do with it!" As it turned out, having "nothing to do with it" even meant refusing to complete financial aid forms for his son (who ended up at a school he did not want to attend).

On the other hand, I find parents who are really selecting a school for themselves and allowing their son or daughter to be spectators during the process. I recall one admissions interview several years ago at which, after I invited the student to join me in my office, the candidate's mother jumped from her chair and insisted, "You'll need to include me in this interview, too!" I informed her that all interviews began with the student alone. Later, I discovered she had shoved her chair next to my closed office door!

For parents, the college selection process can be exciting, puzzling, threatening, and exhausting. The most successful college searches, however, involve the family. That's why more literature, letters, and messages are being directed to *parents* as part of admissions offices' recruitment efforts. With the cost of four years' education totaling somewhere between $40-$80,000, is it any wonder that parents are viewed as a critical element in the college decision?

Of course, parental support during the high school years will help build a solid base for your child's college planning. Some of the groundwork you'll need to do includes finding out the answers to these questions: Are the proper college preparation courses being taken? Has some preliminary career exploration taken place? Is your son or daughter being given opportunities to develop creative, athletic, or leadership skills?

Familiarize yourself with different colleges and universities. Know what they are looking for in applicants. Read college literature thoroughly to assist you and your child with planning a family trip to visit college campuses. Remember that *best,* in terms of the fit between your child and an institution, means that your child should be capable of being the most successful, personally and academically, at the school finally chosen. And enjoy this time with your children. You may be surprised by what you observe.

Last but not least, know this: children do indeed appreciate their parents' involvement and support with this major decision. I've heard this many times, and I hope to hear it again and again.

Daniel C. Walls
Director of Admissions
Emory University, Atlanta, Georgia

Introduction

If you are the parent of a child who may be college bound, this book is for you. Whether your child is an eighth-grader, a high school junior or senior, or last year's graduate who's just beginning to talk about college, this book will help you to help your child to make the many decisions that lie ahead.

Studies have shown that you are the most influential person in your child's college choice—even more influential than his or her teachers and friends. What you say about certain colleges, what you urge your child to consider, and how much you decide you can afford will all strongly influence your teenager's college choice.

So what's your role as a parent? Do you take charge of the whole going-to-college process and steer your child all the way through it, a step at a time? Or do you hold back, telling yourself, "She's a big girl. It's about time she takes some responsibility. If she drops the ball, those are the breaks."

And what about paying for college? How much do you think you can afford to pay for your teenager's education? Should you set some limits on which schools will be considered, based on tuition and other costs, or just let your child apply wherever he wants and see what happens?

You'll need answers to these and other questions. And you'll find them in this book.

We're going to look at everything you, as a parent, need to know about planning for your child's college education:

▶ How much you should get involved

▶ Where to go for the right information

▶ What kinds of questions you should ask

▶ How to get the financial aid to which you are entitled

▶ What the timetable is for every stage in the going-to-college process

As a high school career counselor, I've coached hundreds of parents through this process. In fact, this book is a step-by-step presentation of the most constructive advice I've offered over the years.

There's a lot I want to share with you about helping your son or daughter prepare for college. But I realize you're a busy person. You only have the time to learn what's essential. So here is every parent's guide to the going-to-college process, as simply put and as practical as I can make it.

Let's get started.

CHAPTER 1

Is Your Child College Bound for the "Right" Reasons?

Y ou want the best for your child. Like most caring parents, you've been involved in her education for a long time. You went to the orientation for parents of kindergarteners when she was about five. You went to Parents' Nights at the elementary school. Perhaps you even pitched in when chaperones were needed for a trip to the zoo, or when a seat was vacant on a PTSA committee. You read the teacher's remarks on your daughter's report cards, encouraging her to do better when possible and praising her when she succeeded. All the way through, you've seen it as one of your responsibilities to help your child in school.

Now you and she are approaching a new milestone — graduation from high school — and your teenager is college bound. But you're wondering, Does my child really want to go to college . . . and if so, does she want to go for the "right" reasons? How involved should I get in the many decisions that going to college presents? In this chapter we'll help you answer these questions together.

What Are the Reasons for Going to College?

Any one of several hundred colleges in the United States will grant your child admission once he has received his high school diploma. In other words, higher education is easily within his reach. So, whether or not your child can "get in" is not the issue. More important is *why* he wants to go. Let's look at a typical situation.

I'm the career planner in a suburban high school of 2,400 students, and many parents call me for advice, especially in the fall when seniors are busily applying to college. One day, I got a call from a mother who was in the middle of an argument with

her son. "I refuse to spend thousands of dollars on a college education when he doesn't even know why he wants to go to college,"
she said. "Here, maybe he'll tell you." Her son took the phone. "I
don't know why I want to go," he said. "I just do, that's all." "Did
you hear that?" said the mother triumphantly in the background.

Young people need assistance in articulating their reasons for
undertaking such a major step in their lives. Clarifying her thinking about further education will help your child make sound
choices about which college to attend, and this indication of her
maturity will come across to college admissions personnel reading her application. To pave the way for *constructive* discussion
about her plans, talk to your child about her responses to the
questions beginning on page 5 labeled Self-Appraisal.

Well, how did your child do? If he answered that he does not
plan to go to college or is unsure about his plans, you may wish to
skip ahead and discuss with him the information on page 10, "To
Go or Not to Go (to College): Help for the Uncertain Student."

If, on the other hand, your teenager said she does plan to go to
college, you may wish to discuss with her the areas of study she
found most appealing. This discussion will help you to guide
your child in planning her high school coursework and in choosing a college that offers a suitable program of study.

Now, let's look more closely at the reasons your child gave for
wanting to go to college.

To Get a Better Job

Most professionals in higher education bristle when getting a
better job is cited as one of the reasons for attending college.
They will tell you that career preparation is incidental compared
with the larger purpose of teaching young people how to think
critically. But to most people, a college degree is synonymous
with a higher income, an occupation that offers more opportunities for growth and challenge, and a more fulfilling work life. So if
your child checked this reason, he's taking a practical attitude
toward one of the probable benefits of college. Good for him.

To Learn How to Get Along with Different Kinds of People

A college curriculum introduces young people to a range of
cultures and values. In addition, many colleges seek diversity in
their undergraduate populations to further expand young people's
outlooks. If your child checked this reason, she has touched on
one of the important aims of a college education.

▸ Self-Appraisal

I. What are your future plans?

yes no
☐   ☐   I am planning to attend college.

**If No, complete sections II and IV. If Yes, complete
sections III and IV.**

II. Instead of college, what do your plans include?

☐ Vocational or technical school (noncollege)
☐ Business school (noncollege)
☐ Nursing school (noncollege)
☐ Military service
☐ On-the-job training or apprenticeship
☐ Other (please explain): _____

_____

III. If you're planning to attend college, why do you want to go?

(You may have more than one reason.)

☐ To get a better job
☐ To learn how to get along with different kinds of people
☐ To have fun
☐ To make contacts that may be important later in life
☐ To learn how to think critically and analyze information
☐ To please my parents
☐ Other (please explain): _____

_____

IV. Which areas of study are __most__ appealing? (Please fill in any of your major interest areas that are not listed below.)

☐ AGRICULTURE: agronomy, animal husbandry, fish and
  wildlife management, forestry
☐ BUSINESS: accounting, business management/
  administration, marketing/purchasing, secretarial studies

☐ COMMUNICATIONS: advertising, journalism, radio/TV broadcasting

☐ EDUCATION: art education, elementary education, secondary education, special education

☐ ENGINEERING: chemical engineering, civil engineering, electrical engineering, mechanical engineering

☐ FINE AND APPLIED ARTS: architecture, art, dance, dramatic arts, music

☐ FOREIGN LANGUAGES: French, German, Russian, Spanish

☐ HEALTH PROFESSIONS: medical technology, nursing, occupational therapy, physical therapy, pre-dentistry, pre-medicine

☐ HOME ECONOMICS: child development, clothing and textiles, family relations, foods and nutrition

☐ HUMANITIES: creative writing, history, literature, philosophy, religion, speech

☐ MATHEMATICS AND PHYSICAL SCIENCES: biology, chemistry, computer sciences, mathematics, physics

☐ SOCIAL SCIENCES: corrections, geography, law enforcement, pre-law, psychology, social work, sociology

☐ OTHER: _____

To Have Fun

Having fun is an important aspect of the college experience. Recreation provides a necessary counterpoint to studying. College administrators know this and plan programs that will draw students into the social life of the institution. In fact, one of the main reasons students change colleges is that they are dissatisfied with the lack of things to do and opportunities to have fun.

To Make Contacts That May Be Important Later in Life

Though the business world's network of former college chums isn't as strong as it used to be, college is still one of the key places where the foundations of future careers are laid. Professors serve as references for recently graduated job seekers; classmates tip each other off to career opportunities; students involved in campus activities, such as the college newspaper, later run into each other as professionals in the field. Wanting to make contacts in college is a sensible reason for enrolling.

To Learn How to Think Critically and Analyze Information

To develop thinking skills is the most important purpose of higher education. Throughout your child's school years, even up to the end of high school, most of his learning was closely supervised: the specific information he needed to know was outlined by the teacher, and his progress in class was closely monitored. Not so in college. Good college instructors grade on how skillfully students can solve problems on their own, not just on how much material they know. They will test your child's abilities to organize information and complete work independently.

To Please My Parents

Now we come to the reason some students cite for attending college that, if your child checked it by itself, could spell trouble. You have expectations for your child—she knows this. And she wants to live up to those expectations. So, wanting to please you can be one of her legitimate motives for going to college. But it should never be her *only* motive.

At this point in his life, your child should be seeking independence from you; this rite of passage ushers young people into adulthood. If wanting to please you is your child's sole reason for going to college, he will be putting himself in a dependent position for another four years. Don't encourage this dependency. Help him to clarify his *own* goals. To open up the discussion, have him answer the questions in the following section beginning on page 8 called *Clarify Your Educational Goals and Values.*

If your child has completed this questionnaire and is still unclear about her educational goals, vocational and educational counseling are available from a number of sources, including:

▶ high school guidance offices

▶ career planning and placement offices at colleges

▶ placement offices at vocational schools

▶ vocational counseling agencies

▶ counseling services offered by community organizations and professional consultants

▶ Clarify Your Educational Goals and Values

1) What interests and abilities do you have?

☐ ACCOMMODATING

Accommodating people means providing service for them. You might find yourself working in a restaurant, hotel, movie theater, or on an airplane. The hair care and beauty field is another profession where you accommodate others.

☐ ARTISTIC

Do you enjoy music, art, or literature? Someone who is artistic enjoys self-expression. Artistic careers include directing or performing in drama, music, or dance; modeling clothes; using your hands to create or decorate products; writing articles or books; evaluating other people's creative works.

☐ BUSINESS DETAIL

Are you accurate and organized? Perhaps you'd enjoy working in an office setting and being responsible for record keeping, computing, billing, or business strategy. If you prefer working with people, you may wish to meet the public, talk on the phone, or supervise other office workers.

☐ HUMANITARIAN

Perhaps you're a person who gets satisfaction from helping others with mental, spiritual, or physical needs. People in humanitarian fields include nurses, therapists, counselors, and teachers. These are fields where being concerned about others' welfare is important.

☐ INDUSTRIAL

Do you enjoy doing concrete, organized work and knowing exactly what you're supposed to accomplish? Industrial careers are usually found in a factory setting, where workers have close contact with machines and tools. You may be supervising others or counting, inspecting and weighing things on your own.

☐ MECHANICAL

If you enjoy applying mechanical principles to solve practical problems, this could be the field for you. Careers include engineering, repair work, construction, technical problem solving, and other work involving machines, tool, vehicles, and buildings.

☐ PLANTS AND ANIMALS
Imagine working in forestry, farming, or fishing. You may
be taking care of animals or doing physical work outdoors.
You might even own or operate a farm or a florist shop.

☐ PROTECTIVE
Security is the key word in connection with this career field.
People whose job is to keep property and valuables secure
are often in law enforcement, firefighting, or security sys-
tems management.

☐ SCIENTIFIC
Discovering, collecting, analyzing, and problem solving are
typical elements of scientific work. People in medicine,
mathematics, and research have a scientific interest. In these
careers you may be working in a laboratory, helping people
or animals, or checking scientific equipment and procedures.

☐ SELLING
If you're good at persuading people, you might enjoy a career
in sales. Salespeople are found in stores, sales offices, or
even customers' homes. Or you may wish to buy and sell
products at a profit. Sales work also includes advertising
and promotion.

2) **What do you see yourself doing 5 years from now?** ____

_____

_____

3) **Where do you see yourself in 20 years?** _____

_____

4) **Rank the following career values 1–8 according to their
importance to you:**
____ ALTRUISM: Altruism is the career theme of people
whose life satisfaction comes not from what they accomplish
for themselves, but from the act of helping others.
____ CREATIVITY: You would like to have a job in which you
can use your imagination and be inventive.
____ FAME: If being famous is important to you, perhaps you
would like to see your name in the newspaper, on the cover of
a book, or on television. You would enjoy being recognized
wherever you go.

_____ MONEY: In your life, money may be placed ahead of other considerations such as job security and personal interests.

_____ POWER: Is one of your ambitions in life to be a person who controls or has a direct impact on other people's lives and actions? Then having power is one of your goals.

_____ SECURITY: If this is your aim, then you are probably not an adventurous kind of person and would prefer a career that offers little risk.

_____ SOCIAL INTERACTION: You must enjoy working with people rather than by yourself if social interaction is your career focus. You should be friendly and have an outgoing personality.

_____ VARIETY: You are not a person who likes to do the same thing all the time. You are most happy when your activities— whether on the job or during leisure time—offer a good deal of variation.

▶ To Go or Not to Go (to College): Help for the Uncertain Student

Suppose that after self-examination and discussions with you, your teenager discovers that he is unsure that he really wants to attend college. What can you do to help him come to a decision about his plans? You can start by helping him clarify the reasons he is feeling uncertain about college. Two of the most common are:

Personal goals may overshadow academic ones. Graduation from high school offers thrilling opportunities to taste new freedoms. Some students aren't eager to harness themselves to more schoolwork immediately. As a result, they place independence above academics for the time being and postpone any further education.

Teens may want to experiment with other situations. Not all students see college as the pot of gold at the end of the rainbow. Some prefer to roll up their sleeves and go to work right after graduation. Others may feel that a college degree represents more education than they want now, and they enroll instead in a vocational/technical school or an apprenticeship program. The military attracts a substantial number of young people, too.

If your child does want to continue his education, but is wondering whether or not college is the best route to take, help him get the facts about possible alternatives. Instead of having a vague idea that the grass may be greener outside of college, he will then be able to commit his full energies and enthusiasm to carrying out his plans and justifying them.

While a full discussion of alternatives to college is not within the scope of this book, you and your teenager can start by discussing the following educational options:

▶ Alternatives to College

Vocational/Technical Schools

Approximately 105,000 people graduate each year from schools accredited by the National Association of Trade and Technical Schools. In two years or less, your child can learn the basics of any of 94 careers. For a free handbook about accredited schools and their programs, write:

> National Association of Trade and Technical Schools
> 2251 Wisconsin Avenue, NW
> Washington, DC 20007

The Military Option

The United States Armed Services offer a greater variety of technical, vocational, and apprenticeship programs than do civilian schools. Also, the Armed Services provide financial assistance for qualified veterans who want to attend college.

Incidentally, in case your daughter is thinking about enlisting, be aware that the outlook for women in the Armed Services is steadily improving. Today, women make up about 10 percent of total military personnel; about 8 percent of all officers are women.

Apprenticeship Programs

Apprentices learn on the job and through classroom instruction. Most programs take from two to five years to complete. The best source for information about apprenticeship occupations is the *Occupational Outlook Handbook,* available in your child's high school guidance department or in school or public libraries.

▶ How Much Should You Get Involved in Your Child's Planning?

If at this point your child is sure that she wants to go to college, she should now have a clear understanding of *why* she wants to attend—in other words, she should now have some goals to guide her selection of a college.

Many decisions still lie ahead, however, and perhaps you're wondering how much influence you should exert at this point. Being an adult and your child's parent, you probably have an almost instinctual feel for what would be best for your child— but should you speak up?

There's no need for you to keep mum. One of your goals in this process should be to let your adolescent gradually take more and more responsibility for his future, but granting him total autonomy—dumping the situation in his lap, so to speak—is not a good idea. Your child may not be ready to make choices like this, and a laissez-faire attitude on your part will increase his anxiety.

So discuss your teenager's plans with him, imagine possible scenarios, figure up the costs. This is the only way to bring the future into focus. However, read this list of parental DON'Ts first.

DON'T try to relive your dreams through your child. You may wish that more honors or experiences of a certain kind had come your way in life, but don't attempt to take another swipe at these things through your child. It would put too much pressure on him. By the same token, try not to steer him toward the campus of your alma mater just because that's where you were happy. Let him search for the institution that's best for him.

DON'T let decision-making turn into a power struggle. Decisions as important as these can turn into a reenactment of old parent-child tug of wars. Many parents see this stage in their child's life as the last chance to exercise authority. Instead, ease up; let your son or daughter take the wheel as much as possible. Remember, the goal is to decrease your child's dependence on you.

DON'T imply that the wrong decision on your child's part will "hurt" you. Using guilt as a lever is not constructive. Even if you get your way against your child's wishes, you invite a lot of resentment as a result.

DON'T let your child take the line of least resistance. Some young people, rather than undergoing any sincere self-contemplation, will survey teachers, friends, and family members asking, "What would be best for me?" Having gained a consensus, whether or not they really agree with it, they'll go in the recommended direction for the sake of preserving the peace. Such an approach results in the teenager feeling, "This decision was pushed on me by my parents, society, everyone." Allowing your child this "easy out" is antithetical to the purpose of higher education. Encourage your child to take a good, hard look at herself and speak her mind. Your role is to show approval when she shows a desire to seek new challenges in the name of personal growth.

From this point on, I'm going to assume that you and your child both understand and agree on her reasons for wanting to go to college and her educational goals. Good for you! There's still plenty of work to be done, however. And as the first step in planning for college, the next chapter outlines exactly what your child should be doing to make a smooth transition between high school and higher education.

CHAPTER 2

Starting the Countdown to College

There are a great number of actions to take and deadlines to meet as your teenager prepares for college. How will your child remember which standardized tests he needs to take, and when to register for them? When should you and your child schedule visits to college campuses? How soon should you begin applying for financial aid? The following timetable will help you and your child keep track of the important steps to be taken during the countdown to college.

The timetable's chronological organization is meant to provide a useful guideline, though you and your teenager may wish to adapt it to your individual situation with the help of your high school guidance counselor. Please note that the timetable contains several charts that you may wish to refer to on an ongoing basis. A separate College Application Checklist is included at the end of the timetable, for convenient reference.

Post the timetable and checklists in a location where both you and your son or daughter can refer to them. Most young people will need parental supervision to ensure that they meet all deadlines and fulfill all the necessary tasks, but encourage your child to take primary responsibility for following the timetable. As items are completed during freshman, sophomore, junior, and senior year, they should be checked off. This will make precollege planning more manageable, and you'll be able to monitor your child's progress as he or she moves step-by-step toward successfully enrolling in college.

▶ College Preparation Timetable

Freshman Year

Winter

☐ Arrange initial meeting with high school counselor to discuss academic planning for college.

Sophomore Year

Fall

☐ See high school counselor at beginning of term to review college preparation plans for the coming year.

▶ At competitive high schools, a significant number of sophomores take the Preliminary Scholastic Aptitude Test/ National Merit Scholarship Qualifying Test (PSAT/ NMSQT) in October. Counselor can give you information.

Winter

☐ Meet with counselor to review college preparatory course selection.

▶ Try to build up weaker areas; avoid easy courses.

▶ Inquire about taking Advanced Placement courses (see Glossary for definition).

Junior Year

Fall

☐ Sign up for and take Preliminary Scholastic Aptitude Test/ National Merit Scholarship Qualifying Test, which is given in October (the PSAT/NMSQT is also the qualifying test for the National Achievement Scholarship Program for Outstanding Negro Students and the National Hispanic Scholar Award Program).

▶ Work through sample questions provided with the explanatory materials in the *PSAT/NMSQT Student Bulletin*.

☐ Check class rank based on grade-point averages for freshman and sophomore years.

☐ Have parent-child discussion on tentative college plans.

☐ Meet again with counselor to review college preparatory course selection.

☐ Evaluate your participation in extracurricular activities.

☐ Start exploring information about colleges. You'll need to find out about the following:

▶ Application procedures   ▶ Course offerings
▶ Entrance requirements   ▶ Faculty composition
▶ Tuition and fees   ▶ Accreditation
▶ Room and board costs   ▶ Financial aid
▶ Student activities

☐ Make ongoing use of the following chart to record the names of colleges in which you are interested and the admissions tests they require or prefer (consult your school counselor or find out from an authoritative college directory such as *The College Handbook*). This information will help you decide which tests should be taken (some students take both the ACT and the SAT because of the range of colleges they plan to apply to; see Chapter 7) and will help you to complete the **College Application Checklist** at the end of this timetable.

Name of College	SAT	ACT	College Board Achievement Tests
1.			
2.			
3.			
4.			
5.			
6.			

☐ Find out about scheduled college fairs and college nights.

The next scheduled college fair or college night is _____,
                                                      (date)
at _____, in _____.
    (time)   (location)

☐ Attend presentations made by visiting college representatives
(notices are usually posted outside guidance area).

Winter

☐ Register for the Scholastic Aptitude Test (SAT) and
Achievement Tests which are offered several times during
the winter and spring of junior year. If planning to apply
for early decision, complete required tests by the end of
junior year.

☐ Examine financial resources and gather information about
financial aid.

Sources of financial aid include the following: businesses, colleges, foundations, labor unions, government agencies, ethnic
organizations, veterans' organizations, fraternal organizations,
religious organizations, high school organizations, and civic
organizations.

Spring

☐ Register for the American College Test (ACT), which is usually taken very late in the junior year or in the fall of the senior
year.

☐ Begin narrowing down college choices.

1. _____   4. _____
2. _____   5. _____
3. _____   6. _____

☐ Apply for on-campus summer programs for high school students (check the guidance office for posters and information
about these programs; also see Appendix A).

☐ Visit college campuses.

☐ Confer with college counselor to review senior year course
selection and graduation requirements.

Senior Year

July, August, September

☐ Write to chosen colleges requesting application forms, catalogs, and information about financial aid.

▶ Most colleges require that families requesting financial aid provide a Financial Aid Form (FAF).

☐ Check registration dates for fall ACT and/or SAT if retaking either test.

☐ Check progress in fulfilling application requirements (use College Application Checklist at the end of this timetable).

▶ If applying for early decision, begin preparing application no later than August or September.

▶ Obtain necessary recommendations.

▶ Give counselor any forms that must be completed at least two weeks before they are due.

☐ Set goals for grade-point average (GPA) and class rank for the remainder of the year. Colleges look unfavorably on falling grades.

October, November, December

☐ Confer with college counselor to review final-semester course selection and graduation requirements.

☐ Make arrangements for personal interviews with college admission offices if required.

☐ Mail completed college application forms (send them by certified mail to make sure they arrive, and keep a copy of all documents).

▶ All applications and a copy of high school transcript should be sent to the colleges by winter recess.

January

☐ File Financial Aid Form (FAF) or Family Financial Statement (FFS).

   ▶ Check college catalog to see which one or ones are preferred.

   ▶ Forms are usually available in the high school guidance office.

February

☐ Ask counselor to send first semester's grades to colleges if this hasn't already been done.

March

☐ Keep track of correspondence with financial aid agencies.

☐ Combat "senioritis" by getting involved in new activities or setting new goals.

April, May, June

☐ Keep track of acceptances, denials, and financial aid awards.

☐ Reply promptly to colleges that offer admission (you do have the right to delay reply until you've received notification from other colleges you've applied to, or until May 1, whichever comes first).

☐ Submit promptly deposits required for admission and housing at college you will attend.

The checklist that follows will help you to stay on top of the many steps and deadlines involved in making application to colleges. Refer to Chapters 9, "Applications That Open Doors," and 12, "Getting Accepted . . . or Accepting Denial," for a detailed description of the elements in this process.

▶ College Application Checklist

College	1	2	3	4	5	6
Application sent						
Official transcript sent						
Achievement Test scores sent (*if required*)						
ACT scores sent (*if required*)						
SAT scores sent (*if required*)						
Letters of recommendation requested						
Letters of recommendation received by colleges						
Letters of acceptance/denial/ wait list received						
College notified of intent to enroll						
Letters sent to notify colleges not selected						
Health, housing and other forms submitted to chosen college						

CHAPTER 3

The Importance of Your Child's High School Coursework

The most important and influential piece of paper in your child's college application file will be his or her high school transcript, which lists the courses taken and the grades received. The transcript is an academic resume, a record so important to admissions committees that it's generally the first document they look at—the linchpin of a student's application.

After all, a recommendation by a teacher is based on experience in one or two courses. Personal essays by candidates can be written in several days. Admission tests are meant to be completed in just a few hours. And even a face-to-face interview with an applicant can be as brief as 20 minutes. But a transcript takes four years of high school to build. To the skillful reviewer it may say, *This student seems motivated.* His courses were challenging and his grades reflect his ability. Or it may say, *This student seems lazy.* His test scores are high, but he took easy courses and didn't do especially well even in those. It may also say, *This student evidently didn't know what he should have taken to prepare for college.*

Any coursework this important should be prepared with the advice of a professional: your child's counselor.

▶ Counseling

Your Child's High School Counselor

Make a point of meeting with your child's school guidance counselor as early as possible and no later than the end of her freshman year. Many freshmen are required to take a set schedule of courses, so sophomore year may be your teenager's first opportunity to exercise some choices. Plan to continue meeting regularly with the counselor throughout your child's high school career. Don't worry about being regarded as a pushy parent. Counselors prefer that parents take an active role in a student's precollege planning. By doing so, you will be knowledgeable about your child's progress, and you and the counselor can develop rapport.

There are certain things your child's counselor can do to assist you and your college-bound child, such as:

▶ locate information your child will need to register for admission tests.

▶ help plan a schedule of classes each semester.

▶ make information about colleges available.

▶ evaluate your child's performance in light of her possible college choices.

▶ help you learn about the financial aid process.

Do bear in mind that selection of high school courses and all the essentials of the college application process—filing the application, meeting deadlines, keeping up with correspondence— are ultimately you and your child's responsibility, not the counselor's. The counselor's responsibility is to help students explore, clarify, and make the necessary decisions for themselves.

There's a practical reason for you and your teenager to take primary responsibility for conducting the college search: your child's school counselor has many diverse students to guide through the admission process.

The typical counselor's responsibilities are becoming increasingly fragmented. In some schools he might be designated as a kind of "jack-of-all-trades" around the school, serving as part-time truant officer, study hall proctor, or bus duty attendant. Also, like most counselors, he probably has a case load that exceeds, perhaps greatly, the recommended 250 students. And then there's the paperwork to be done. A recent survey of 1,000 counselors showed that 28 percent of their time was devoted to paperwork and administrative and supervisory activities.

Second, the amount of time devoted to college-related counseling varies widely from school to school. Another survey, involving 1,100 high schools, indicated that 40 percent of guidance counselors at upper-income schools spend at least half their time on college counseling, whereas only 6 percent of counselors at lower-income schools spend that much time counseling college-bound students.

For your own use in monitoring your child's coursework, informing yourself about the school's offerings, and keeping a record of what you discuss with your child's counselor, you might wish to bring in the following Counselor Appointment Form each time you visit. The components of this form are very similar to the records counselors maintain about students.

▶ A Sample Counselor Appointment Form

Counselor's name _____

Phone number _____   Office hours _____

Sophomore Year

Date _____

What are the high school's graduation requirements?

Course	Credit(s) Required	Credits to Date
English	_____	_____
Mathematics	_____	_____
Science	_____	_____
Physical education	_____	_____
Social studies	_____	_____
Academic electives	_____	_____

Are Advanced Placement courses available?   ☐ Yes   ☐ No
In which subjects? _____

_____

Is my child in a college preparatory program? ☐ Yes   ☐ No

Which courses should my child take this year and next to increase
his or her chances of acceptance into the program of his or her
choice at a college or university? _____

_____

Will my child meet with his or her counselor a specified number
of times?

      ☐ Yes   ☐ No

How do students make appointments to see their counselor? ___

_____

_____

What percentage of the students go on to college?

Two-year _____   Four-year _____   Total _____

Does the school offer a course that prepares students for
college admission tests? ☐ Yes   ☐ No

When should my child sign up for the Preliminary Scholastic
Aptitude Test/National Merit Scholarship Qualifying Test
(most students take it in October of the junior year but some
take it in sophomore year)? _____

Junior Year

Fall

Date _____

What is my child's class rank? ___ in a class of ___

Where is information about colleges available in the school?

When will college representatives visit the school?

The next scheduled college fair or college night is _____,
                                                    (date)

at _____, in _____
    (time)   (location)

Which courses should my child take this year and next to increase
his or her chances of acceptance into the program of his or her
choice at a college or university?

Junior year: 1. _____   Senior year: 1. _____
             2. _____   2. _____
             3. _____   3. _____
             4. _____   4. _____
             5. _____   5. _____

Winter

Date _____

How can my child do a scholarship search at school?

Is my child fulfilling the graduation requirements and taking the
courses we discussed earlier? ☐ Yes ☐ No

If no, for what reasons? _____

Spring

Date _____

Which colleges should my child be considering?

1. _____   4. _____
2. _____   5. _____
3. _____   6. _____

How can my child find out about on-campus summer programs
for high school students? _____

What are the registration deadlines for:
the American College Test (ACT)? _____
the Scholastic Aptitude Test (SAT)? _____

Senior Year

Fall

Date _____

What is my child's class rank? ____ in a class of ____

Should he retake the SAT or the ACT? ☐ Yes ☐ No

Reasons: _____

_____

Is my child fulfilling the graduation requirements and taking the courses we discussed earlier? ☐ Yes ☐ No

If no, for what reasons? _____

_____

Winter

Date _____

When will financial aid forms be available, and where can they be picked up?

Have my child's seventh-semester grades been mailed to colleges he applied to?

    ☐ Yes ☐ No

Working with an Independent Counselor

If for some reason you think that your child needs help that requires more time than the school counselor can reasonably provide, you can investigate the services of an independent counselor.

Independent counselors have been around since the Depression, when private colleges were badly in need of students. At that time, some institutions paid independent counselors a fee of approximately 10 percent of the tuition for every student they placed. That is not the way independent counselors—often calling themselves educational consultants—work today. They collect their fee from parents; as a result, they work on behalf of the student and her parents rather than on behalf of any institution. A one-time consultation usually costs $100-$250; an extended, step-by-step program may be priced anywhere from $750-$1,250.

To find an independent counselor, request a list of names from:

Independent Educational Counselors Association
128 Great Road
Bedford, MA 01730

When contacting a recommended counselor in your area, ask for a list of qualifications and several references. Also, make sure you understand what kinds of services he or she will offer and at what cost.

During a one-time consultation, for example, the counselor may meet briefly with your family and then spend some time alone with your teenager, after which she will conclude with some recommendations. If you're seeking more extensive help, she may offer to meet with your family, administer tests to your child, make referrals in certain situations, and assist you in communicating with educational institutions. She may also advise you about preparation for admission tests and even assist your child in filling out applications. Many independent counselors keep in touch with clients long after a student they've counselled has been accepted, in case some follow-up work is needed.

But be aware that the same caveat applies whether you're working with an independent or a school counselor: don't think you can leave it all in the counselor's hands. Filing applications, keeping track of credit requirements, and meeting deadlines is still the responsibility of you and your teenager.

When you meet with an independent counselor, it's a good idea to have a copy of your child's transcript with you. Counselors use a student's transcript, and what it indicates about overall grade-point average and rank in class, as the foundation for their recommendations. Rather than estimate what grade your son or daughter received in geometry last year, request a copy of the transcript in advance from the school registrar.

Probably the first recommendation a counselor will make during your initial meeting with him (preferably during your child's sophomore year) will be that your child take a pattern of coursework that will satisfy the requirements of most colleges. Let's take a look at that pattern.

▶ High School Coursework for the College-Bound Student

Basic Requirements and Strategy for Electives

Although few colleges insist on a specific pattern of high school courses, many have certain basic requirements. A typical four-year math sequence is plane geometry, algebra, advanced algebra and trigonometry, and calculus. Many colleges prefer four years of English. In fact, when 1,463 institutions were surveyed recently about their preferences, four years of English was the "most common and uniform requirement among all categories of colleges." Between one-third and one-half reported requirements in mathematics, natural sciences (biology, chemistry), and social sciences. The least common requirement was foreign language coursework, which was expected by fewer than one-quarter of the respondents. Some preprofessional programs, such as those for medicine, engineering, and architecture, may require certain sequences of math or science.

A pattern of coursework that will meet the requirements of most institutions includes:

▶ four years of English

▶ three years of math (two of algebra, one of plane geometry)

▶ two years of science (biology and chemistry, plus physics if your child is considering a science-related profession)

▶ two years of history

▶ two years of a foreign language

Electives, however, are a little bit trickier. The best advice for choosing electives was neatly summarized by a guidance department colleague of mine who said, "Stick to meat and potato courses." That is, stick to courses that are academically challenging. College admissions personnel want to be confident of two things: that the candidate under consideration has challenged herself and has taken full advantage of what her high school has to offer, and second, that she has successfully equipped herself with the intellectual skills necessary to handle college-level work.

But what if your child still has room for electives and it's a toss-up between taking a third year of French or a fourth year of math? The rule is simple: your child should try to stick with elective coursework that will improve her grade-point average and her rank in class, and/or is related to her academic areas of interest. I'm often asked, for example, whether or not a student should take a third year of foreign language. I first ask, "How are you doing in second-year language studies?" If the response is "Not so hot," I inquire next whether the student plans to major in some field requiring foreign language. Usually she will say no, since wise students plan to study in academic areas where they are strongest. So my advice is, "Forget the third year of language and substitute a challenging course in which you can excel." After all, if a student has been in a college preparatory program like the one outlined above, there's no point in taking electives that might bring down her grade-point average. She should capitalize instead on her strengths.

Incidentally, there's a widespread myth that colleges hardly look at an applicant's last-semester coursework; consequently, some students pack their last semester of senior year with a lot of "breezy" courses (at one Eastern academy these courses are called "gases" as opposed to "solids"). But don't let your teenager fall for this one. Colleges *always* stipulate that their acceptances are conditional pending a review of the applicant's last-semester coursework and grades. I honestly can't say I've heard of a student's acceptance being revoked at the last minute, but why should your child risk it?

Advanced Placement Courses

If your child is fortunate enough to be attending a high school that offers Advanced Placement courses, he might want to enroll in one or more of these courses during his junior or senior year.

Advanced Placement courses provide college-level work for unusually able students. These courses offer the opportunity to earn college credit. A student who's intellectually curious and wholeheartedly interested in a subject can sharpen his study skills in an Advanced Placement course; at the same time, he can learn to cope with the demands of college-level coursework. In addition, his transcript will demonstrate to admissions officials that he can handle courses at the college level. At the end of each Advanced Placement course an optional exam is offered that is scored 1-5. Many colleges grant credit for those courses depending on the student's score. Exams are given in:

American history	computer science	Latin: Vergil
American govern- ment and politics	English language and composition	Macroeconomics Microeconomics
art, history of	English literature	music: listening and
art, studio	and composition	literature
biology	European history	music theory
calculus	French language	physics
chemistry	French literature	Spanish language
comparative gov- ernment and politics	German language Latin: Catullus- Horace	Spanish literature

Reasons Some Students Don't Succeed at College

An important step in helping your child understand why she will benefit from a college education is to bring into focus the degree to which she is prepared for some of the demands of college. One way you and your teenager can approach this question is to discuss the most common reasons that some students do not succeed at college.

Learning takes effort, and grades in high school predict grades in college as accurately as do college entrance exams. If your child is having schoolwork problems but is planning to attend college, he should try to clear up his difficulties now before going on to an environment that will be even more challenging. If his problems are not the kind that can be solved with a little effort, then you and your child may want to consider colleges with special admissions or skill improvement programs for students who need structured help (see Chapter 8).

Keep in mind that only half of the differences in students' educational attainments are attributed to academic abilities. The rest have to do with self-image and motivation.

Adolescents with a poor self-image usually have difficulty in reaching their goals. Feelings of inadequacy, inferiority, and other self-image problems may grow in intensity in the college environment, where competition is rife. If your child has suffered from these feelings for prolonged periods during his school years, address them head-on with the help of a professional such as a school psychologist or therapist.

When it comes to some aspects of college, only motivation will sustain young people and lead them to success. Consider some of these challenges:

▶ Class assignments that require long stretches of studying or research

▶ Questions, posed as topics for papers or projects, which seem to defy answers

▶ A lifestyle requiring adult levels of self-sufficiency

▶ A demanding schedule that may include working full- or part-time, as well as carrying a full load of courses

If your discussion of common potential problem areas indicates academic or nonacademic factors that could stand in the way of your child's success at college, you and she should make an appointment to see the appropriate teacher or your child's counselor. List in advance concerns that you would want to discuss at a conference.

What If High School Course Offerings Are Inadequate?

Sometimes, however, scheduling coursework that will best prepare your teenager for college isn't as easy as simply choosing from a wide variety of college-prep courses. A scarcity of challenging courses might present a major obstacle to your child's college preparation.

If your child has exhausted all the academic challenges that the school can give him, he has two options. One is to enroll in several courses at the local community college or enroll as a part-time student in a four-year college (see Glossary for Early Admission option). The other is to take courses for high school or college credit through correspondence. Both require ambition, a quality that will not be lost on an admissions person (especially if your child makes a point of describing on the application how you and she went the extra mile). To schedule appropriate community college courses, you and your child should make an appointment with a counselor there (see Chapter 5 for further information on community colleges). For correspondence courses, check *The Macmillan Guide to Correspondence Study,* Macmillan Publishing Company, New York, 1985.

What If Instruction Is Inadequate?

If inferior quality of instruction or a lack of challenge are impeding your teenager's college preparation, talk to your teenager and the teacher in question first to find out exactly where the problem lies. Then, if you feel that your teenager is not getting enough academic challenge, arrange to have your child's counselor steer her toward the school's best teachers. A school social worker once introduced a student who wanted to transfer into my honors English class. "Tom has been getting B's in his regular-level English class," she said, "but says the problem is that the course doesn't make him work hard enough." Although this sounded like a contradictory argument to me, I decided to take a chance. As it turned out, Tom led my class; in fact, he was an exceptional boy in many respects, and eventually was accepted at Princeton. So much for my impression of a contradiction. Tom needed challenges.

What Are the Causes of Academic Problems?

What if your college-bound child seems to be having trouble in her classes? First, be sure of the facts before drawing conclusions. Poor marks can indicate immaturity, emotional distress or other personal problems, problems with teachers, or perhaps just bad study habits.

Begin by talking with your teenager. It's best to keep an open mind and not attempt to persuade her into agreeing with your perceptions. Try to get her to clarify what the difficulty might be—personal problems, poor relationships with teachers, or lack of study time, for instance. The final step is to follow up by talking with teachers to set some reasonable goals and devise a plan for reaching them. Assure your child of your concern and your support, and convey optimism about resolving the situation.

Another approach is this: monitor your child's homework and try to get an idea of the standards being set. For example, if your child's algebra assignment consists of 20 straightforward problems, and by 11 p.m. he still hasn't solved half of them, then perhaps you ought to think about whether his struggles are related to any of the four most common impediments to good grades: insufficient study time, too much social life, an academic load that's too heavy, or just a general lack of interest in school.

In any case, follow up by talking with his teachers. Avoid automatically assuming that the school is at fault. I know a principal who likes to tell parent groups, "If you promise not to believe half of what your child says about school, I'll promise not to believe half of what he says about his home life." In other words, wait until you've heard both sides of the story.

If schoolwork is difficult for your child—and even if it is not—try to provide her with an environment at home that is conducive to doing her best. See that she has a quiet place to study, and provide her with reference books and magazines of interest.

But some parents say, "Four years is a long time to keep after my child about school, plus there are a lot of distractions—driving, dating, an afterschool job, and sports practice. Is there one year that's the most important to my child's preparation for college?"

Yes, junior year.

Junior Year and Counting . . .

Junior year is crucial to the college-bound student for a number of reasons. This is the year that admissions officers will expect to see your child hit her stride in school. In other words, she should be enrolled in courses at her level of ability and should be doing well in them. Consequently, it's important to seek a counselor's advice concerning third-year course selection. Both semesters should have a balance of solid college prep classes.

Extracurricular Participation

During junior year, your child should also try to become more involved in extracurricular activities. On a practical level, a student might have trouble landing a spot as a club officer beyond junior year, since other students may already have been moving in that direction for some time. It's also unlikely that he will be a starter on any sports team, because most of his teammates will already have been playing for several years.

From an admissions person's point of view, an applicant who suddenly becomes involved in activities during senior year inspires some skepticism. Colleges prefer applicants whose extracurricular interests have developed over a couple of years, at least. Then again, the well-rounded student who flirts with many activities—a year in band, a semester on the school paper, another year on the swim team—looks noncommittal. Colleges would rather see a second-chair clarinetist who's been in the school band for three years and who's earned her spot as president of Key Club, than the dabbler who's nibbled at many clubs but who has never shown any serious involvement. Encourage your child to follow through on interests.

To give you an idea of the emphasis many colleges put on a high school student's extracurricular activities, here's an excerpt from the Common Application, a form used by 120 colleges and universities:

▶ Extracurricular and Personal Activities

Please list your principal extracurricular, community, and family activities and hobbies in the order of their interest to you. Include specific events and/or major accomplishments such as musical instruments played, varsity letters earned, etc. Please (✔) in the right column those activities you hope to pursue in college.

The chart that follows asks for grade level of participation, and number of hours per week and weeks per year spent on activity, as well as positions held, honors won, or letters earned.

On-Campus Summer Programs

Junior year is also a good time for your teenager to think about spending part of the summer participating in an on-campus program for high school students. Such programs have multiplied tremendously over the last several years. Typical offerings include special science programs, fine arts workshops, natural science expeditions, writing seminars, drama productions, computer camps, and classes for gifted students (see Appendix A for a wider listing). Some of these programs are free, while others can cost over $1,500. The key advantage of these opportunities is that they give students a taste of what it is like to be at college before making a commitment that will cost thousands of dollars. High school students can live in dormitories, hear lectures by professors, meet people from many backgrounds, and compete with students of similar academic ability.

Early Entrance

Some colleges and universities offer Early Entrance, an opportunity for qualified students to matriculate before graduating from high school. Often parents wonder, Should my child, if offered the chance, go directly from junior year in high school to college?

A lot depends on your child's level of maturity. Some students outgrow high school by junior year and are ready to accept the responsibilities and challenges of higher education. Others aren't quite ready and would benefit from another year in high school. In terms of what future employers might think if a young person had entered college early, too few students take advantage of Early Entrance to allow generalizations.

What *can* be said is this: if your child gives any indication that he or she is worried about missing senior year activities — prom, participation in varsity letter sports, graduation with classmates — then it would be better to put off enrolling in college until the normal time. Early Entrance is for students who are emotionally clearly beyond what high school can offer them.

At the very least, the summer of your child's junior year should include several visits to college campuses, if he hasn't done this already. Keep in mind that events move quickly during the fall of senior year; the previous summer may be the last chance to plan visits to colleges before deadlines start crowding in (see Chapter 4 for guidelines on what to see and do when visiting a campus, and on how to choose a college).

Junior year is also the time when students take one or more of the standardized tests for college admissions. Chapter 7 discusses these tests in detail.

How to Make the Right College Choice

O ne day after school as I was straightening up the waiting area in the guidance office, I found a cartoon drawn by a student on a scrap of paper. It depicted a haughty director of admissions leaning against a podium and thinking, "ACT 31 ... SAT 1250"—an illustration, I suppose, of the notion that rigid standards are responsible for determining which students will be admitted to which colleges.

Nonsense. Actually, *self-selection* by students has more impact on the final outcome than do the admissions practices or standards of any institution. As an example of how self-selection operates, take the girl who is first in her class and could be admitted to highly selective schools, but who chooses a local college that is not highly selective, mainly because it's near home. Consider also the boy who is barely in the upper third of his class and would have a better chance at a local college, but who researches all kinds of institutions and finally settles on one that's 2,000 miles away.

Admittedly, these choices are made within limits set by the colleges: how high is tuition and what are the academic criteria. Nevertheless, while college admissions offices hold some of the cards, the key plays are always made by the applicants. Students set their own criteria, exert as much effort as they care to, and end up on one campus out of more than 2,000 available. If colleges were pulling all the strings from the start, students would not have such considerable powers of choice.

For some students, making such major choices—perhaps for the first time in their lives—is intimidating. Young people tend to want to keep all their options open. But learning that this isn't

always possible is part of growing up. As Hannah Gray, president of the University of Chicago, advises:

> Young people should not be afraid to choose a direction,
> even if it means closing some doors. Fulfillment means
> living with the choices one makes, which may be con-
> straining in some ways while allowing freedom to grow
> in other ways. This is as true about one's personal life
> as it is about one's professional life. And women some-
> times need to have this said to them more often, because
> the entire realm of choice and freedom is often a novelty
> to them.

As a parent, you are probably willing to do your utmost to help
your child choose the right college. But keep in mind who is going
to college. Ultimately it will fall to your teenager to adjust to the
institution that's chosen, so begin shifting the responsibility off
your shoulders as early as possible. Your role includes taking an
active interest, providing relevant financial information, and being
a good listener. But sending away for college catalogs, filling out
applications, and mailing off a housing deposit should not fall to
you. Let your child *choose a direction,* as Gray advises, as part
of growing up.

"Well," you might be thinking, "I wouldn't go so far as to send
away for catalogs and applications." But the parents about to be
described probably thought they were keeping out of the way as
much as possible, too.

Bob O'Rourke is a graduate of a large university with a strong
Irish-Catholic affiliation. His oldest son, Bill, graduated from
there, and now his daughter Kathleen is looking at colleges. Bob
has told a few friends that Kathleen will probably attend the
family alma mater, too. But Kathleen is seriously considering two
small liberal arts colleges, and she feels guilty because she thinks
she's letting her father down. The moral: the right college is
where your child will fit in scholastically and socially. Try not to
hold expectations about which school your child will attend. Why
bother to let your child think he's "choosing" if the outcome is
predetermined?

Here's another example of "helping" that isn't really helpful.
Roland Holmes and his wife Amanda were both surprised and a
bit angered when their son Ed, who had always performed well in
the sciences, announced that he was looking for a school with a
good photography department. Holmes phoned Ed's counselor

the next day and tried for 20 minutes to get him to promise that he would "talk Ed out of this nutty idea." From an ethical standpoint, the counselor's first allegiance was to his student and client, and he was not in a position to promise anything. But more to the point, Ed's father tried, through a quick maneuver, to deprive Ed of the experience of choosing a particular kind of school. It would have been more appropriate if Ed's father had phoned the counselor and said, "Would you talk to Ed and try to find out if this is what he really wants?"

Recognize that it takes a lot of courage for a young person to say no to family expectations or to strike out in a direction that others have not anticipated. Young people in their late teens are at a point in their development when they have to test their independence. If college didn't exist, as the saying goes, it would have to be invented, because our society needs some kind of ritual that allows young adults to leave the nest. If you prefer practical reasons to let your child take the reins in the matter of college choice, then think about this: if you compel your daughter to please you by attending a certain institution, and later she fails, not only do you risk recrimination, but your child will inevitably lose some self-esteem as a result of the whole fiasco.

I don't mean to imply that the college search is fraught with peril and that your child is likely to make a mistake. Selecting a college is not much more difficult than, say, buying a home. One of the most important ways to approach the task is to set a positive, optimistic tone that will encourage family members to participate in a helpful way. After all, the advent of a child going to college is a milestone that the family is reaching together.

There are four steps in choosing a college: making preliminary choices; comparing various institutions; making campus visits; and deciding which institutions to apply to. Let's look at them each in turn.

▶ Step 1: Making Preliminary Choices

As was pointed out in Chapter 2, "Starting the Countdown to College," your child should make an appointment to see his counselor about college planning during freshman year. His counselor will have the resources to guide him in any feasible direction toward college he wishes; however, *the more thinking your child does ahead of time about what he wants in a college, the fewer false paths he'll go down and the less frustration he'll experience.* It's ironic, but some students who come to counselors with an attitude that demands, "Tell-me-where-I-should-go-to-college," are often the ones who later complain that they're being pushed into a decision. The best way for your child to ensure that he is really the one making key decisions about his future is to try to make as many preliminary choices about colleges on his own as he can.

Deciding on Distance from Home

One of the first things your child should settle in her own mind is the general location—region of the country—where she would like to attend college: the Middle States, the Midwest, New England, the South, the Southwest, or the West.

When it comes to the location of the college and its distance from the student's home, I generally encourage students to give serious thought to going far away to college. The majority of college students live within 500 miles of the campus they choose. Many of them probably could have been accepted at other schools, perhaps at more challenging schools in some cases, but the appeal of being within 'laundry range' of home immediately ruled out three-fourths of all the possible choices. My advice is to read up on more schools that are farther away and see what's out there.

On the other hand, going far away results in higher transportation expenses. The cost of a year at a far-flung college has to include trips back and forth between campus and home for holidays, birthdays, and other occasions. Also, being far away means that homesickness may pose a problem. Coming home for weekends usually isn't possible.

For these reasons and others, many students are perfectly happy living at home and commuting to college. This arrangement is less expensive, often offers a better chance of landing a part-time job, and usually entails fewer adjustment problems. Perhaps the greatest value of commuting is that it allows students to test the waters at college with a lower degree of risk.

Commuting also has its disadvantages, but with a little effort, these can be overcome. For example, students who commute usually don't get very involved in campus activities, because most social events are held after class and on weekends. While it may be inconvenient to come all the way back to campus after dinner for a meeting at the Student Center, the student who makes an effort to get involved with on-campus activities can prevent the experience of going to college from turning into a grind that offers little social benefit.

Statistics indicate still another problem—that students who commute tend to do less homework and fail more classes than their noncommuting classmates. One possible explanation is that commuting students experience some lack of commitment because they feel like outsiders on campus. Loneliness, too, can sometimes be a problem for the commuting student because he feels "out of it" compared with students living on campus. Again, the best remedy is to get involved in campus activities, make friends with classmates, and resist the temptation to socialize exclusively with old high school chums. One more problem that commuters may have to contend with is that it can be difficult to create a schedule of classes without time gaps that leave them hanging around on campus.

It's not hard to improve the experience of commuting as long as you and your child discuss all its aspects up front. For example, will she start paying board? Who will provide transportation? If your daughter goes out with friends after an exam, will it be all right to come in at 2:00 a.m.? These may seem like mundane matters, but it's from tiny aggravations that mighty misunderstandings grow.

As you can see, distance is an important aspect of college choice. Before your child decides whether to go to college nearby or far away, discuss this point with her.

Considering Admissions Selectivity

After distance, the next determinant of your child's college choice should be the admissions selectivity of each college. Some colleges have standards that few applicants can meet. Others welcome all high school graduates, regardless of their grades or test scores. Surprised? Let's explode a long-cherished myth about grades and admissibility right now: *a child doesn't need good grades to go to college.* Just by having a high school diploma, he can be admitted to more than 700 two-year and

130 four-year colleges. If he has a C average, he will be considered at another 1,000 institutions. A B average will give him a chance at all but about 200 colleges and universities. Moreover, the odds are in his favor that he will be admitted to the college of his choice. A recent survey showed that 92 percent of students get into their first or second choice college. So if your child is already worrying at the tender age of 17 or 18 about missed opportunities due to mediocre or poor grades, tell him all is not lost—not by a long shot. He still stands a good chance of getting into a college that meets his needs. If he has set his sights too high for his current qualifications, he can consider starting at a two-year community college. Improving his academic skills there in order to transfer to a four-year college is an effective way to resolve the problem. In the meantime, he should concentrate on pulling up his grades and developing good study habits in his senior year of high school.

At this point in her research—the point at which she is required to do some close reading of admissions standards expressed in test scores and class rank—your teenager will need to consult a college handbook. It will pay for itself many times over by saving time and money. One that is updated annually and recommended by many counselors is *The College Handbook*, published by the College Board. It includes detailed descriptions of some 3,000 two- and four-year colleges and contains a number of indexes to help locate specific information such as colleges for men or women only; campus environment; open admissions colleges; Common Application colleges; college application priority and closing dates; colleges with late or no closing dates; and colleges with special admissions programs.

Generally, colleges and universities have one of four admissions policies:

Open (all high school graduates are accepted until the entering class is filled to capacity)
Liberal (some accepted applicants are from the lower half of their high school class)
Selective (the majority of applicants are in the top 25 percent)

Highly Selective (the majority of applicants are in the top 10 percent)

When your child is looking at an institution's range of test scores submitted by accepted applicants, a useful rule of thumb is that her scores should not be in the top or bottom 15 percent. In the first instance, the college may not be challenging enough for her; in the second, it may be too challenging. *She should be about in the middle.* The same rule of thumb holds true for overall grade-point average; but take into consideration the standards of your child's high school. A private metropolitan school may demand more of its students, for example, and your child's rank would be higher were not the students so competitive.

Keep in mind that colleges want their students to succeed. An admissions committee looks for applicants who will be intellectually challenged and at the same time able to achieve their goals in the academic environment of that particular college.

Evaluating Academic Offerings

Next, your child should weigh the programs offered by each college or university in making his choice. Unfortunately, college handbooks provide only a starting point in this area. They merely list an institution's programs or majors like entrees on a menu: accounting, agricultural business, applied art, biology, business administration, commerce, etc. In addition, however, your teenager can gather clues from other sources as to the caliber of instruction in several fields, by determining whether the institution has chapters of Phi Beta Kappa, the honor society for liberal arts students (see Appendix B for the list of the 237 colleges and universities with chapters of Phi Beta Kappa); Sigma Xi, the honor society for science students; and Tau Beta Pi, the honor society for engineering students. These organizations grant chapters only to institutions of proven academic strength.

This initial information is helpful to a young person with a notion of what he would like to study. But to thoroughly investigate course offerings and the actual coursework involved, which is the backbone of any degree program, your child should send away for the school's own catalog. He can do so with a brief letter, as shown below.

Bill Jonson
1345 Neenah Drive
Butler, PA 60430

> Mr. Daniel C. Walls
> Director of Admissions
> Emory University
> Atlanta, Georgia 30322

July 8, 1986

Dear Mr. Walls:

I am a junior at Middletown High School. My ACT score
was 29 and my SAT scores were 550 verbal and 610 math.
I am in the top 10 percent of my class, and I am especially
interested in biology and genetics. Please send me a
catalog and application materials. Thank you.

> Bill Jonson
> 1345 Neenah Drive
> Butler, PA 60430

There are good reasons for including these details. First, there
may be a special publication just for juniors; second, the scores
will alert Mr. Walls to scholarship opportunities for Bill; third,
mentioning his areas of interest might elicit a special brochure or
pamphlet about study opportunities in that field at Emory
University. And fourth, catalogs are sometimes not sent unless specifically requested.

   In about two weeks, your child will receive a packet of information designed especially for applicants, including the catalog.
This will usually resemble an oversized paperback book. No
other publication contains as much detail about the college as its
catalog. Unfortunately, most students don't read catalogs: first,
because they look imposing, what with all the fine print about
degree requirements and credit hours; and second, because they
make for such dry reading. In fact, a survey of 42 college catalogs
rated the reading levels of all of them at *difficult* to *very difficult,*
and concluded that readers virtually need a college degree to
fathom them. Nevertheless, the catalog constitutes the authoritative statement of what an institution offers.

The table of contents will refer your son or daughter to such information as:

▶ admission requirements   ▶ living facilities
▶ academic programs   ▶ student services
▶ degree requirements   ▶ special programs
▶ the faculty   ▶ social, cultural, and
▶ the calendar   religious information
▶ costs and financial aid   ▶ general information

Concerning programs of study, a university—and remember that a university is partly made up of separate colleges—will list them under each college: College of Business and Commerce, College of Liberal Arts and Sciences, etc. A four-year college, however, will refer your child directly to programs of study by major—agriculture, education, home economics—to cite a few examples. In general, private colleges and universities offer fewer major fields of study than do public institutions because part of the mission of public institutions is to serve a broader student population.

While examining programs of study, two important things to look for are *accreditation,* and *breadth and depth* in the range of courses offered.

Checking for Accreditation of Programs of Study

Accreditation indicates that a college or a degree program has met certain minimum standards for its program of study, staff, and facilities. If your child plans to graduate as a chemist, a musician, or some other specialist in the arts or sciences, she should find out whether the program or college has professional accreditation. Some examples of accrediting organizations are the American Association of Bible Colleges and Schools, the Association of Independent Colleges and Schools, the National Association of Schools of Music, and the National Association of Schools of Art. Usually a school's catalogs will say whether the institution has been accredited in some area. If the catalogs are not helpful, consult the latest edition of *Accredited Institutions of Postsecondary Education* (Middle States Assn. of Colleges and Schools, Philadelphia, PA), available in the high school guidance office or in public libraries. If there's still no indication of accreditation at an institution your child is considering, she should call the admissions office and find out the reason. Sometimes the review procedure for accreditation is lengthy, and the "seal of approval" could be pending.

Evaluating Breadth and Depth of Programs

Next, your child should judge the breadth and depth of programs of study that appeal to him. In a program of wide breadth or scope, your child would have the opportunity to specialize in one area of a much broader subject. A discipline such as the study of English literature, for instance, would be approached from many different perspectives. Indications of this would be availability of courses about the history of the language, its structure, its various forms—prose, poetry, and drama—and the individual histories of those forms, as well. Depth, on the other hand, is marked by the opportunity to enroll in at least two advanced courses in a major field: one of them a regular classroom course and the other listed as a seminar, independent research, or honors course. Programs offering advanced standing, as it's called, will expose your child to material usually covered in graduate courses, which is a fitting conclusion to undergraduate study.

Reviewing Faculty Credentials

Your child should review the credentials of the faculty as closely as an employer would examine the resumes of job-seekers. Colleges and universities are usually proud to list the degrees of their faculty members and where they were granted. How many of your child's potential instructors have a Ph.D.? Where were they educated? Diversity is important in this case: too many instructors recruited or hired from the same alma mater is not a good sign. Also, does the catalog list their scholarly or professional accomplishments? English majors may want to be taught by published writers and critics, physics majors by active researchers, and political science or government majors by instructors who have served in posts related to that field. Likewise, business majors may want to learn at the hands of men and women who are former executives or practicing consultants.

Considering an Institution's Size

Next, after making some choices about distance, admissions selectivity, and program offerings, your child will probably want to look at colleges and universities of a certain *size:*

▶ Very small (under 1,000 students)

▶ Small (1,000–3,999 students)

▶ Medium (4,000–8,999 students)

▶ Large (9,000–19,999 students)

▶ Very Large (over 20,000 students)

Size is really a matter of personal preference. A child who has enjoyed having close relationships with his teachers would probably prefer a small school where instructors make themselves accessible to students. A self-directed child, on the other hand, might be happy at a large institution. Following are some pros and cons of small vs. large schools that your child might want to keep in mind:

Small Schools

Pro	Con
▶ Admissions process likely to be more personal	▶ More emphasis on fitting in
▶ Closer relationship with faculty	▶ Fewer instructors to choose from
▶ A sense of belonging	▶ Less privacy, fewer new faces
▶ Activities easier to participate in	▶ Fewer activities to choose from
▶ Less competition for courses	▶Fewer courses to choose from

Large Schools

Pro	Con
▶ Greater diversity in student body	▶ Greater risk of anonymity
▶ Greater range of faculty and facilities	▶ Less supportive atmosphere
▶ More extracurricular activities	▶ More competition in which to participate
▶ More opportunities to exercise independence	▶ More problems with "red tape"

Later in this chapter we'll discuss visiting colleges, which can help your child see how differences in size affect the atmosphere of various campuses.

Considering Social Opportunities

In my experience, a student's preference for institutions of a certain size usually indicates something else—what kind of social activities he likes. A teenager who zeros in exclusively on large universities usually looks forward to attending football games featuring powerhouse teams, and celebrating the outcome of the game back at the 100-member fraternity house (to this day, my wife, who attended the University of Michigan, orders everyone to be silent when football scores are being announced on the radio or TV, and cheers a Michigan victory). Not so for the student who isn't keen on a "rah-rah" atmosphere and looks with disdain on the social characteristics of large universities. College handbooks describe the social activities available on every campus, but again, once your child has opted for institutions of a particular size, it will be important that she visit them to see whether her impressions are confirmed. Small may seem too small and large too large after she's had the chance to visit.

Deciding Between Coed and Single-Sex Schools

Along these lines, your child will also have to make a decision about the type of student body he prefers, coed or single-sex. Some young people assume that single-sex colleges offer a narrower range of social activities than coed schools. And studies have indeed shown that students who attend single-sex colleges usually express some dissatisfaction about the social life. But as I point out in Chapter 5, there seems to be an interesting trade-off at women's colleges in particular: the absence of men on campus results in more opportunities for involvement and leadership. According to surveys, students at women's colleges tend to have higher aspirations for themselves—perhaps because they enjoy greater opportunities to head committees and organize activities.

Considering Financial Aid

And now for the biggest "bugaboo" connected with choosing a college—cost. College handbooks break down the cost of attending an institution into tuition, fees, room, and board. But you must add in how much your child will need to cover additional expenditures such as travel, books, clothing, and spending money. In most instances, this will average out to an extra $1,500 or slightly more per year. Already I detect the butterflies in your stomach as you think about paying "full freight" for your child's college education. But help may be forthcoming, through financial aid.

"Financial aid?" you retort. "We make too much money to be considered for financial aid." I'll bet that's precisely what the families in the following examples thought, as well.

At Rockhurst College in Kansas City (MO), 67 families with incomes of $60,000 or more applied for financial aid for a recent academic year. Twenty-five of those families, or 37 percent, were awarded aid that averaged $2,736. At Brandeis University in Boston, families with incomes of more than $70,000 have applied for and received financial aid based on demonstrated need.

The point is that making cost one of the major considerations at the outset may be putting the cart before the horse. Factors such as the number of other children you may have in college, the size of the mortgage on your home, whether or not you have regular medical bills, and a host of other aspects form, in the eyes of financial aid administrators, an aggregate profile that might surprise you! So while you might like to give your child a ballpark estimate of what your family can afford for college, you may be limiting your child's choices more than is necessary. My advice is to encourage your child to settle on half a dozen institutions *without regard to cost,* and then wait and see whether or not each school offers you financial aid and in what amounts. At that point, you and your child can decide which of the schools that have accepted her are affordable (how to apply for aid is discussed in full in Chapter 11, "Everything You Need to Know About Financial Aid").

As a way of summarizing some of the internal decisions your child has made about the types of colleges or universities that appeal to him, here is a checklist to record his preferences:

▶ Checklist for Choosing Colleges

Geographic location

☐ Middle States
    Delaware
    District of Columbia
    Maryland
    New Jersey
    New York
    Pennsylvania

☐ Midwest
    Illinois
    Indiana
    Iowa
    Kansas
    Michigan
    Minnesota
    Missouri
    Nebraska
    North Dakota
    Ohio
    South Dakota
    West Virginia
    Wisconsin

☐ New England
    Connecticut
    Maine
    Massachusetts
    New Hampshire
    Rhode Island
    Vermont

☐ South
    Alabama
    Florida
    Georgia
    Kentucky
    Louisiana
    Mississippi
    North Carolina
    South Carolina
    Tennessee
    Virginia

☐ Southwest
    Arkansas
    New Mexico
    Oklahoma
    Texas

☐ West
    Alaska
    Arizona
    California
    Colorado
    Hawaii
    Idaho
    Montana
    Nevada
    Oregon
    Utah
    Washington
    Wyoming

☐ Large city   ☐ Small city   ☐ Suburbs   ☐ Rural
☐ No preference

Admissions Policies and Practices

☐ *Open* (all high school graduates are accepted up to capacity)
☐ *Liberal* (some accepted freshmen are from the lower half of the class)
☐ *Selective:* (the majority of the applicants are in the top 25 percent)
☐ *Highly Selective* (the majority of applicants are in the top 10 percent)

Curriculum

Course of study:

☐ Liberal arts   ☐ Business
☐ Engineering   ☐ Fine arts
☐ Preprofessional   ☐ Technical
☐ Teacher training   ☐ Other

Special Programs

☐ Honors program

☐ Study abroad

☐ Academic skill-building program (help for students with resolvable learning difficulties)

☐ Phi Beta Kappa chapter (honor society for liberal arts students)

☐ Sigma Xi chapter (honor society for science students)

☐ Tau Beta Pi (honor society for engineering students)

☐ Graduate courses open to undergraduates

Academic subjects you enjoy in high school: (1) _____
(2) _____ (3) _____

Profession or field of study you intend to enter: _____

Enrollment Size

☐ Very small
   (under 1,000 students)
☐ Small
   (1,000–3,999 students)
☐ Medium
   4,000–8,999 students)

☐ Large
   (9,000–19,999 students)
☐ Very large
   (over 20,000 students)

Campus Life and Intercollegiate Sports

☐ Archery
☐ Badminton
☐ Baseball, softball
☐ Basketball
☐ Bowling
☐ Cross-country running
☐ Equestrian sports
☐ Fencing
☐ Field hockey
☐ Football
☐ Golf
☐ Gymnastics
☐ Ice hockey
☐ Lacrosse

☐ Martial arts
☐ National or local fraternities
☐ National or local sororities
☐ Riflery
☐ Rugby
☐ Sailing
☐ Skiing
☐ Squash
☐ Swimming & diving
☐ Tennis
☐ Track & field
☐ Volleyball
☐ Water polo
☐ Wrestling

Type of College

☐ Two-year college
☐ Four-year college
☐ University or
   four-year college
   with graduate
   work

☐ Public
☐ Private (not
   church-related)
☐ Private
   (church-related)

☐ Coed
☐ Men only
☐ Women only

▶ Step 2: Comparing Various Institutions

Now that your child has some preferences to work with, it's a good idea for him, or both of you, to attend a college fair where you can compare institutions. College fairs are usually held on week nights in high school gymnasiums, shopping malls, or exhibition halls. They usually attract local, regional, and national institutions.

When you arrive at a college fair, get a list at the door of the institutions being represented, and check off which ones are "must sees," based on your child's initial criteria. Incidentally, some people think that if they haven't heard of an institution, it can't be very good. But consider that most people can name only about 20 colleges at most, and there are more than 3,000 in the United States. Quite often, a school's visibility is due to its age, or its athletic teams, or its close proximity to one's home. None of these attributes by itself is reason enough to choose one school over another.

A revealing way for your child to compare colleges at a fair is to ask their representatives or alumni to answer the same questions. Incidentally, you'll notice I said *your child* should ask the questions: many of the representatives who attend college fairs also review applications and conduct interviews at their own institutions. If you immediately take over the questioning, the representative might assume that your child hasn't got the *chutzpah* to act on his own. And admissions people have an uncanny way of remembering these kinds of things. Here are some key questions your child should ask:

▶ What is unique about your institution?

▶ What type of students are happiest at the college?

▶ What type of students usually succeed there?

▶ Which departments are considered to be the strongest?

▶ What are the most popular majors? Why?

▶ What percentage of classes are taught by professors, and what percentage by teaching assistants?

▶ Do most students graduate in four years? How many do not?

▶ What percentage are from outside the college's immediate vicinity?

▶ What fraction are black, Hispanic, Jewish, etc.?

▶ What's the male-female ratio?

▶ What fraction of students leave campus for the weekend?

▶ Where do students live after their first year: in dormitories, in fraternity or sorority houses, off campus?

▶ What intramural sports are available?

▶ What support services are available to students?

▶ Are computers available to undergraduates?

Listen to what representatives tell your child, and afterwards share with him your impressions of the fair. It's too early for you to begin expressing preferences for certain colleges, however. Try to leave the field open for your child as long as possible. If at the outset you encourage a dialogue about choosing a college, hopefully the trend will continue and your son or daughter will seek your advice from time to time.

By now, your child should be down to a few choices, and should have examined their application materials and catalogs. It's time for both of you to visit the campuses of colleges and universities that deserve the closest look possible.

▶ Step 3: Making Campus Visits

Timing and Parental Involvement

As a parent, how involved should you get at this point? Let's take an example.

Phil's father is doing a great job of helping his son choose a college. So when I heard that he was going to tour several campuses with Phil, I asked what the two of them planned to see.

"Oh, shoot," he said, "I'll probably just stay in the hotel room. I don't want Phil to think I'm looking over his shoulder. It's his decision, you know." I often hear this kind of remark from parents. They want to help as much as possible, but when it gets down to the wire and their son or daughter is visiting campuses, that's the time parents think they should keep mum.

Actually, your involvement is as essential as ever. Not that you should force your impressions of a college on your son or daughter, but when visiting campuses you should examine an institution in light of your child's welfare. After all, going to college is a major step involving a young person's future goals, his self-esteem, and even his safety. Considering the emotional and financial investment that you and your family are about to make, your parental perspective at this stage can go far toward ensuring that your son or daughter makes a successful transition from high school to higher education. You won't be overstepping your role as a parent if you visit a college with these concerns in mind. Your child needs your insights at this vital and thrilling moment in his or her life.

Let's look at the timing of your visit, how to prepare, and what you should do and see when accompanying your child on a campus visit.

As Chapter 2, "Countdown to College," indicates, it's not necessary or even advisable to wait until senior year to start visiting campuses—you're likely to initiate a mad scramble to try and see everything in a short space of time since most applications have to be filed by late fall. A better idea is to begin touring campuses as early as you can. If your child hasn't done any searching yet, take a drive to a nearby college to attend a football game. This need not be an institution that your child is even considering. Just use the game or some other activity—a presentation by a well-known speaker, or an exhibit on campus—as an opportunity to get yourself and your child accustomed to the college environment. You might include a couple of campuses as stops on a family vacation.

But if your child has done his research and is prepared to look over a few final choices, arrange to visit these institutions during the regular school year, rather than during summer vacation, if possible. This timing will enable you and your child to see the campus in full swing, not when it's partly deserted and the school's personality is temporarily out of sight. Other times to avoid scheduling a visit are on special days, such as "Mom's Days," homecoming, or some other campus celebration. Although these are exciting events, once again they're not typical, and won't present a realistic portrait of the campus as it appears most of the time.

Attending an Open House

One kind of event that can be very helpful, however, is a campus open house or visitation day. The purpose of these get-togethers is to acquaint you and your child with many aspects of the college in a short space of time. You'll be invited to informal gatherings where you'll have the opportunity to talk with students, faculty,

and administrators. In addition, there will be tours of the fac
and, perhaps, some cultural program such as a play or cor
Consult the college's catalog for dates of open houses, or pl
the admissions office.

If you opt instead to visit on an ordinary school day, write or
phone the admissions office at least two weeks in advance. You
will be invited to take a tour of the campus conducted by student
guides, and you can also make arrangements to stay overnight in
the dormitories or at the student center. Before leaving for a
campus tour, your child should obtain a copy of her high school
transcript and a profile of her high school—the school's parent-
student handbook will do, for example—and she should take a
portfolio of her work if she's considering a major in fine arts. It's
not unusual to meet the director of admissions if you make an
appointment for a tour, and your child might be interviewed on
the spot, so she should be prepared.

Now here's a list of what you and your child will probably
want to see on campus:

▶ Art galleries
▶ Athletic facilities
▶ Bookstore
▶ Classrooms and lecture halls
▶ Computer facilities
▶ Dining facilities
▶ Dormitories
▶ Fraternity and sorority houses
▶ Language laboratories
▶ Library
▶ Music practice rooms
▶ Radio and TV stations
▶ Religious centers
▶ Science laboratories
▶ Student center
▶ Theatrical facilities

Some of your goals while on campus will be the same as your
child's: to tour the campus, ask questions about financial aid, talk
with students, and generally soak up a feel for the campus. But I
also recommend that you spend time away from your child,
investigating those aspects that interest you as a parent.

For example, your child's welfare will depend in part on the
caliber of support the institution has to offer. These include the
student counseling offices, the health services, and the career
placement office. At each of these places, find out how a student
makes an appointment and what kind of services are available.
For example, does the counseling center offer walk-in appointments for students who need advice or counseling immediately?
What if your child becomes ill—how extensive are the health
services and what does student insurance cover? When your
child begins thinking about employment after graduation, will he

have the opportunity to be interviewed by recruiters at the career placement office? Are seminars offered on resume-writing, job-hunting, and interviewing skills? An evaluation of these kinds of services will give you an idea of the extent to which an institution contributes to the total development of its students.

If you have questions about the college that you'd prefer to discuss privately, make an appointment to see the dean of academic services. He or she can answer questions about academic probation, changing majors, counseling service, and penalties for breaking various rules. The dean will be willing to share advice about what your child will need to do to succeed at the college, and how you can be supportive as he or she faces academic and emotional challenges.

Another good resource is the students themselves. Don't think you're imposing by asking what they think of the college and what advice they would have for a new student. Most are happy to share their experiences.

And if you haven't done so already, buy a copy of the student newspaper and look for other current issues on campus. Don't expect to read that nothing exists except sweetness and light between the administration and the students. After all, higher education teaches students to think critically and to analyze issues. But a student newspaper that seems filled with apparently unresolved complaints about apathy, antagonism, and even crime is a warning sign.

By now it's time that you and your child compare notes. Although your child's impressions are very important—he's the one who will have to adjust to the institution—your parental concerns deserve attention, too. Try not to convey pessimism, if that's your attitude, but point out any problems you may foresee that your child will ultimately have to consider.

As an adult, your opinion of a campus may differ from your child's, who probably has his own priorities in mind. For example, you might be concerned over the noise in a dormitory, while your son or daughter might interpret this as the hallmark of a fun place to live.

As a method of sharing your impressions as equals about a campus you visited, try using an objective system of evaluation. Together make a list of places you visited—the student union, a classroom, the cafeteria. Then separately, and without any discussion, rate each place on a scale of 1-5 with one being "unacceptable" and 5 being "acceptable." After you've finished, average the scores for each entry on the list. Any entry that receives *less* than a 3 deserves to be discussed more fully. This system lets you focus in on any areas of mutual concern. Try not to sabotage the purpose of the evaluation system by insisting that your opinion is the only correct one, or that your child is unqualified to make judgments. After all, once she arrives at college, she will face many decisions without the benefit of your advice, so encourage her independence now.

▶ Step 4: Deciding Which Colleges to Apply To

If your child has done the work outlined in this chapter, he will probably want to apply to half a dozen colleges (see Chapter 9, "Applications That Open Doors") that represent the best possible choices. Having winnowed down his field of possibilities by tabulating his preferences at the outset, then adding to his decision-making ability with more information, then comparing one institution against another, and finally visiting campuses whose appeal remained strong, he will have done his best to investigate the opportunities. There will continue to be positives and negatives, of course, about each of his final selections—Utopia University has yet to be established. But the crucial part of making the right college choice is doing the necessary research in advance.

In the next several chapters, you will see how the work he does on his applications can make a big difference in whether or not admissions officers offer him acceptance. Which college he ultimately chooses to enroll in, however, may depend on which school offers him the best financial aid package.

CHAPTER 5

Big University/Small College: What's the Difference?

P icture a college. What do you see? A big brick building with colonial windows and white pillars? Or perhaps a grassy quadrangle with students studying beneath some trees? Or a classroom with a white-haired instructor writing formulas on the board?

These are all typical scenes inspired by the word *college*. But go a step further. Is your college public or private? Is it denominational (church-related) or nondenominational? Is it a two-year or a four-year school?

Don't worry if you aren't able to visually add these characteristics to your imaginary college. You could visit 10 campuses and not see any visible clues to distinguish one type from another. But the differences are there all right, and your child should consider them carefully as he begins his college search. One very basic difference, for example, is the distinction between a college and a university.

Colleges and Universities Defined

Generally, a college is an institution of higher learning that grants a bachelor's degree after four years of study. Many students beginning their search are unaware that there are two kinds of four-year colleges. First there's the liberal arts college, which offers a cultural education through four years of study covering the arts, humanities, and social sciences. Students begin to concentrate during their third year on what they have selected as their major field of study—political science, literature, or biology, for example. The majority of liberal arts colleges are private and enroll fewer than 5,000 students.

The other type of four-year college is more specialized. These institutions put less emphasis on a broad liberal arts education, offering instead, more preparation for a specific career in education, engineering, music, art, business, and other fields. They, too, are often small- to medium-sized institutions.

A university, on the other hand, encompasses a liberal arts college, separate undergraduate programs such as engineering or business, and various graduate programs that grant Master's (M.A.) or Doctor of Philosophy (Ph.D.) degrees. In addition, universities usually include graduate professional schools in such fields as law, architecture, and medicine.

Small Colleges vs. Large Schools

Representatives of small colleges like to advertise that "small is better." To a high school student, assurances of a warmer, more personal atmosphere, smaller classes, and more individual attention are very attractive. And it's true that small colleges may offer a better chance to participate in extracurricular activities, because fewer students there are competing for spots. Also, the kinds of instructors who settle in at small schools generally tend to enjoy teaching more than research.

It's tempting, of course, to reverse all the positives of a small school and assume that the opposite must be true of large institutions: that classes are bigger, hence they must be more impersonal, and so on. But let's not ignore what large schools (those with more than 10,000 students) have to offer by virtue of their size. Large schools offer more courses to choose from, a greater range of extracurricular activities, greater diversity among students and faculty, more lab facilities, a greater number of famous faculty members, and more opportunities for research and graduate study. A big selling point among students is that large schools afford more privacy. As a student attending a Big Ten university said to me, "What I like is that you have your circle of friends and you go your own way—period."

The College Consortium

An arrangement blending all of what large and small schools can offer is the college consortium, an agreement by a group of schools that allows students to use the resources of all the member institutions. Cross-registration is usually permitted, so that students can do their lab work at the schools with those facilities, for example, while another member institution reciprocates by opening all of its liberal arts courses to students in the consortium. A well-known Eastern consortium in Massachusetts has as members Amherst College, Mount Holyoke College, Hampshire College, Smith College, and the University of Massachusetts.

The Two-Year Alternative

So far, all of the institutions described have been four-year schools. However, if your child isn't ready to make a commitment of that length but still wants a college education, then she should consider a two-year school.

There are approximately 1,200 two-year colleges in the United States, of which 85 percent are public schools. The states with the most two-year schools are (not in order) California, Florida, Illinois, Michigan, New York, Texas, and Washington.

Public two-year colleges were established to meet the needs of a diverse student population—urban, rural, non-native born, etc.—and to help these students decide on their educational and career goals. In many states, public two-year colleges are required to accept all high school graduates who are residents of the state or of the school district.

The strength of the public two-year college system is its versatility. It offers three kinds of education. The first leads to a two-year associate degree, not transferable to a four-year institution. These "terminal" degrees are available in nursing, police science, real estate, secretarial science, dental hygiene, and many other areas. The second kind of associate degree program educates students as though they were freshmen and sophomores in a four-year system. After graduating with a two-year associate degree in liberal arts, business, English, mathematics, or journalism, for example, these students can transfer to a four-year institution and receive a bachelor's degree after two additional years of study. And the third kind of program trains students in a particular career field so they can seek immediate employment after graduation. Certificates, not degrees, are awarded for completed work in such fields as air-conditioning, child care, word processing, and tool and diemaking. Some certificate programs are as short as two or three months, and some span a year or more.

The advantages of attending a two-year college are substantial, although it's been my experience that students tend to scorn anything that's in their backyard. Near my home is a community college that students used to refer to by sarcastic nicknames. One of the nicknames stuck and eventually became a term of affection. Now students at the college wear T-shirts saying they attend "Harvard on Halsted Street." Nevertheless, community colleges offer low tuition, the chance to combine part-time work with schooling, and the opportunity to "test the waters" of college while still living at home.

Understand, however, that if your teenager goes the community college route with the intention of transferring to a four-year school, he must take a *university parallel curriculum*. This means that his freshman and sophomore courses must satisfy the requirements of the college he plans to attend. This isn't hard to accomplish, but many transfer students lose a semester needlessly by neglecting to do a little research in advance. Your child should study the catalog of the four-year college carefully and talk with an admissions counselor there to make sure he's taking courses that will transfer. One hitch is that four-year colleges vary in the kind and amount of transfer credit they will accept. Another problem has to do with converting quarter-hour credit, granted by some two-year colleges, to semester hours at another institution (a headache too involved to describe here). But by taking a little care beforehand, transfer students can save themselves a lot of frustration.

One final bit of advice: your teenager should apply for admission to the four-year college by October or November of her sophomore year at the community college. Transfer students have to abide by the same deadlines as all other applicants. If she waits until she has graduated to apply, she may find herself denied admission until mid-winter.

Public vs. Private

What's the difference between a public and a private college education? If you say cost, you're like most people. Actually, private colleges want to attract students from diverse income levels, so they offer competitive amounts of financial aid to stay more competitive with the costs of public education. The most meaningful difference between public and private colleges has to do with the reasons they were founded.

Private colleges were founded to meet the goals of various religious denominations or were organized along lines laid out by progressive thinkers of the day. Antioch College (OH), for example, founded in 1852, is one of the oldest innovative liberal arts colleges in the country. Its first president, educational reformer Horace Mann, pioneered such ideas as coeducation, nonsectarianism, and nonsegregation. Public institutions, on the other hand, were founded to meet the manpower needs of the states that established them. This difference in mission continues to influence the character of private and public higher education. And as your child conducts his college search, he will probably be influenced by the "feel" of one kind of higher learning over the other.

The two strongest appeals that public institutions offer are these. First, they're less expensive because they're partly or fully supported by taxes. And second, public colleges and universities are, on the whole, much less choosy about whom they accept. Less than 25 percent of the selective and highly selective institutions of higher learning in America are public.

Private colleges tend to be more selective for two reasons. One is that they believe they can enhance the experiences of some students by introducing them to an environment where certain standards of performance are expected. A student who has shown evidence of enjoying intellectual challenges may flourish, for instance, in a private college's freshman-level seminar where everyone is expected to contribute and to complete a self-designed project. The second reason is that getting the "right kind" of student—one who will speak well of the institution and perhaps even become a staunch and generous supporter of the "old school"—is vital to the college's survival. Both ends are served—academic atmosphere and survival—by carefully reviewing each applicant's file and accepting only those who seem to be a good match with the college. Many students who apply to private women's colleges, for example, do so in the belief that these institutions offer opportunities for intellectual and personal growth not available elsewhere.

Private Women's Colleges

Women's colleges have existed for more than 150 years. Miss Pierce's Academy, founded in Connecticut in 1792, claimed to be the first. But it was not until 1837 that Mount Holyoke College officially became the first college exclusively for women. The first female college president, Ada I. Howard, took the helm at Wellesley College (MA) in 1875.

Until the 1960's, women's colleges generally prospered, but

then rising costs and the women's movement made all-female institutions seem outdated and, ironically, sexist. Today, women's colleges remain outwardly the same. They are small, enrolling only a few hundred to a few thousand undergraduates; they are residential, and between one-third and one-half have ties to the Roman Catholic Church.

But philosophically, women's colleges have broken with their image as expensive finishing schools. Instead, they strive to stay on the leading edge of what modern women are seeking in their personal and professional lives, often with more sensitivity to women's individual development than their coed counterparts. Alverno College (WI) emphasizes "The capacity to see and think from a variety of perspectives, to weigh evidence and to formulate sound conclusions, to apply creative solutions to complex problems—these are the abilities that today's woman will need for effective management of her personal and professional life." Mundelein College (IL) holds regular "weekend colleges" for women employed in business. Marymount Manhattan (NY) has a day/night year-round curriculum for female job-holders and those beyond the usual college age. And Simmons College (MA) conducts a special 10-week institute for women in middle-management who are seeking promotion.

Beyond simply tuning in to what women want to learn, women's colleges offer a unique social environment. One young woman describes it this way: "I'm comfortable being around women all day. I don't need to 'dress to impress,' because I'm not competing for boyfriends. And I talk more in class, because there are no men to think I'm too smart or too dumb. I'm really getting the chance to enjoy being female." Students at women's colleges can also benefit from closely interacting with female instructors, administrators, and campus leaders—role models whom many young women find inspiring.

Black Colleges and Universities

The value of role models is also worth considering in connection with historically black colleges. Before the Civil War, most blacks had been denied even a rudimentary education, so that by 1860 the number of black college graduates in the United States stood at only 23. After Emancipation, through the efforts of church and missionary groups, black colleges began to appear. A century later there were 15,000 blacks in historically white colleges in the South, the "separate but equal" doctrine of education having been abolished by the U.S. Supreme Court in 1954. Today there are 107 predominantly black colleges—39 public and 68 private. Most of these were founded during the period when black colleges stood apart from the white system of education.

Students who attend black colleges find satisfaction in the following:

▶ Enrollment is usually small.

▶ Most of the school's activities—social and service groups—are targeted at attracting blacks.

▶ Career counseling is attuned to the backgrounds of the students.

Whether a college is predominantly black or white, your child should visit the campus, talk with the students, and evaluate the institution in the ways described in Chapter 4.

Denominational Schools

By far, the largest number of private colleges in the United States were founded through the efforts of a particular church group. Many of these schools have since severed their religious ties, among them Northwestern University (IL), The University of Redlands (CA), and Whittier College (CA). Although nearly every denomination has had a role in establishing private colleges, the majority were founded by Roman Catholic missionary bishops in this century to serve immigrant populations.

Currently there are 350 Catholic colleges and universities in the United States, varying in size from an enrollment of 13,000 at Loyola University in Chicago to the six full-time students at St. Basil's College in Stamford, Connecticut. Most are concentrated in the Northeast and North Central sections of the United States. Despite the high visibility of the Catholic Church in service-related projects around the world, however, the career choices of students who attend Catholic colleges are not significantly different from those who attend nondenominational institutions.

One place where your child undoubtedly would feel the presence of religious teaching is at a Protestant Evangelical college such as Oral Roberts University (OK). Here the authority of the administration is not only academic, but moral and spiritual as well. Oral Roberts' catalog warns against "unseemly behavior," which includes "sexual immorality, cheating, lying, stealing, gambling, profanity, vandalism, use of alcoholic beverages and tobacco, improper dress, violation of the rights of others, and all other negative forces."Attendance at chapel services is required twice a week; three unexcused absences result in automatic cancellation of a student's enrollment.

As a general rule, however, the amount of influence that a denominational college or university has on the behavior and attitudes of its students is something that the individual applicant has to judge. Take Illinois College, for example. This Christian college has ties to the United Presbyterian Church and the United Church of Christ. Students are required to take two courses in religion, one of which must be about the Bible. But as former Director of Admissions Marti Clark points out, Illinois College retains mainly historical ties with its sponsoring church: "Our student body is almost 40 percent Roman Catholic, and only 7 or 8 percent Presbyterian," she says. "Being one of five Presbyterian colleges in Illinois, we're not nearly as close to the church as, I would say, Alma College, which is the only Presbyterian college in the state of Michigan."

Would a student really notice the differences between a denominational institution like Illinois College and one that's nondenominational? Says Clark, "The only way to tell is to visit the campus and see for yourself." Another way to get insights into denominational schools is to talk to students, faculty, and university representatives who have some experience with them (see Chapter 4 for college evaluation techniques).

As you can see, the differences between private and public colleges are—if you'll pardon the pun—partly a matter of degree. But if this chapter has led you to wonder how you and your child will introduce yourselves to the various types of higher learning out there, the next chapter on recruitment demonstrates that colleges and universities are eager to share information about themselves. For now, let's finish with a rundown of popular nicknames associated with some colleges and universities, both public and private:

▶Nicknamed Groups of Colleges/ Universities

The Big Ten

Big Ten schools are both public and private, selective and highly selective. Though it's hard to make generalizations about ten institutions that have a combined enrollment of over 250,000, these universities are distinctive for offering comprehensive curriculums that are strong in many areas. When Britain sought to revamp its system of higher education after World War II, several of the model institutions it studied were Big Ten schools.

The Big Ten is composed of the following institutions: the University of Illinois, Indiana University, the University of Iowa, the University of Michigan, Michigan State University, the University of Minnesota, Northwestern University, Ohio State University, Purdue University, and University of Wisconsin.

The Service Academies

The United States Service Academies are highly competitive institutions that offer superior educational opportunities. If your child has a desire to attend one of the academies, he or she must:

▶be a citizen of the United States

▶ be at least 17 and not more than 22 years old during the year of admission

▶ be in good general health

▶ be unmarried

▶ be of good moral character

▶ have completed high school or its equivalent

▶ be nominated by a member of Congress, or another nominating authority (the Coast Guard Academy does not require this kind of nomination)

For more specific information about the various requirements for application to each academy, write:

United States Air Force Academy
Colorado Springs, CO 80840

United States Coast Guard Academy
New London, CT 06320

United States Merchant Marine Academy
Kings Point, Long Island, NY 10204

United States Military Academy
West Point, NY 10996

United States Naval Academy
Annapolis, MD 21402

The Ivy League

The Ivy League Colleges are a group of scholastically prestigious institutions located on the East Coast. Since they are among the most selective institutions in the country, your child should consider them if she:

▶ Is in the upper 10 to 20 percent of her class

▶ Has participated in a variety of extracurricular activities

▶ Scores anywhere from 600 to 800 on both portions of the SAT

The Ivy League consists of Brown University, Columbia University, Cornell University, Dartmouth College, Harvard and Radcliffe Colleges, Princeton University, University of Pennsylvania, and Yale University.

The Seven Sisters

Seven additional schools that are also recognized as being scholastically prestigious are The Seven Sisters. Admissions requirements to these institutions are generally the same as those of the Ivy League schools.

The Seven Sisters are Barnard College (Columbia University)**, Bryn Mawr College, Mount Holyoke College, Radcliffe College (Harvard University), Smith College, Vassar College, and Wellesley College.

**Allows cross-registration between the two campuses.

CHAPTER 6

No Salesmen Will Call (Maybe): What Your Child Should Know about Recruitment Strategies

One brisk fall morning a couple of years ago, I flew into Des Moines on a visit to a well-known university there. I toured the campus with about 30 other high school counselors, and we were shown the dormitories, the library, the gymnasium—places that would add to our favorable impressions of the school. I noticed, however, that the buildings and grounds seemed to show signs of financial strain. So at lunch I asked one of the admissions people whether this was true.

"Well," she said, putting her fork down slowly, "we're depending a great deal on tuition revenues these days. We can't plan more than a couple of semesters in advance..sort of like living from paycheck to paycheck."

Most people are probably unaware that higher education, despite its promises of a better life and a higher standard of living for its graduates, is itself pinching pennies these days and struggling to keep the wolf from the door. Already, many leaders in higher education are being forced to agree with the attitude of one admissions analyst who says, " . . . we are, after all, businessmen in that our business is producing and selling education."

The reason for this reversal of events is, simply, that there are fewer students of college age now than a decade ago. A decline in the number of young people who will populate most of the colleges during the next 20 years clearly forecasts that college enrollments may drop 10 to 40 percent between now and the middle of the next decade. During the 1970s, more than 100 American colleges closed. Some experts predict that another 100 to 400, most of them small liberal arts colleges, may close by the year 2000. What this means to your teen-

ager is that during her college search, she will be the target
of many kinds of recruiting strategies.

From a college's viewpoint, recruitment refers to the various
means by which colleges make their programs and services known
to potential students. From your son's or daughter's perspective,
it means receiving lots of mail, possibly a few phone calls from
colleges, definitely some invitations to open houses on campuses,
perhaps even a visit to your home by a local alumnus. And if your
child is a particularly appealing candidate—an academically talented student, an athlete, or a member of a racial or ethnic minority
—you can expect colleges to double their recruitment efforts.

It's a heady experience for a young person to be courted this
way. The sudden change from just being an adolescent to being
the recipient of personal letters from directors of admission can
be very flattering. But keep in mind that your child must look
beyond the invitations and phone calls to that first day when she
starts as a freshman at the college of her choice. By then all the
hoopla will have ended, and she should be content with her
decision. That's the goal, that's what matters most.

Actually, college recruitment is nothing new. Since 1643,
when Harvard issued a promotional tract entitled "New England's
First Fruit," colleges have been trying to get students' attention.
Around 1900, colleges began using brochures and catalogs to
give students glimpses of things that might attract them—the
campus' appearance, the cost, programs of study—factors that
students still consider in making their choices. But in the early
1970s, when the problem of declining enrollment first surfaced,
colleges began supplementing their recruitment efforts with a
technique long known to business—marketing.

For instance, during the heyday of the ecology movement in
the late sixties and early seventies the University of California at
Santa Cruz tried to capitalize on its beautiful seaside campus by
mailing applicants viewbooks with photographs of students sun-
bathing, strolling along the beach, and hiking in nearby forests.
Among the university's administrators this practice was derisively
nicknamed "selling the redwoods." Not every college can offer an
attractive campus, of course, but each can emphasize aspects of
itself that at first glance look very appealing. There are many
ways of "selling the redwoods," sometimes making it hard for
students and parents to separate a school's image from reality.

Some colleges' marketing efforts—monogrammed Frisbees,
T-shirts with slogans, a juggling act inside a shopping mall—are
relatively harmless and even entertaining. One college was plan-

ning to release hundreds of balloons carrying announcements of scholarship opportunities until it was learned that the local residents were equipping themselves with bows and arrows!

Deceptive Marketing Practices

A few institutions' marketing efforts are not harmless, however. Some have used deceptive practices to lure potential applicants. An Indiana college's promotional materials showed a photograph of a couple standing near a waterfall, though there is no waterfall on campus. Photographs have also been improperly used to make subtle, deceptive impressions—to picture scenes portraying more minority students than actually attend the school, or undergraduates using equipment that's not usually available to them. Rumors circulate that some schools pay their recruiters a headhunting bonus for every student they enroll. Finally, a few institutions have not been above lying, by offering financial support that never materializes or promising privileges that are never actually extended.

All of this illustrates that college-bound students have considerable market power. In fact, the "bidding war" for candidates has become so heated—witness cocktail receptions for students and parents, personal phone calls from faculty members, alumni pressure, promises of summer jobs—that a majority of high school counselors in one survey predicted an increasingly important role of theirs will be protecting students from aggressive recruiting practices. Perhaps the best advice for you and your child was stated in the title of a booklet distributed by the former U.S. Department of Health, Education, and Welfare: *Helpful Hints for Selecting a School or College: Look Out for Yourself.*

As a college applicant, your child should expect:

▶ to be informed by a college of all of its policies concerning fees, refunds and financial aid awards.

▶ that classes will be conducted at the times and locations scheduled.

▶ to defer responding to an offer of admission until hearing from all institutions to which he or she has applied, or until May 1—whichever is earlier.

▶ to be free from discrimination.

▶ to have access to facilities—laboratories, dormitories, dining halls—that are equal to those in other parts of the campus.

▶ to have access to adequate student services: counseling, job placement, and extracurricular activities, for example.

If your child is denied any of these things, contact his college admissions counselor and ask for the address or phone number of the state or regional president of the Association of College Admissions Counselors. Or write to:

Executive Director
National Association of College Admissions Counselors
1800 Diagonal Road, Suite 430
Alexandria, VA 22314

Recruiting Methods

Now let's look at the various methods of recruitment your teenager is likely to encounter. The four most popular means of recruiting students are through mailings, visits to high schools by representatives, college fairs, and phone calls.

Recruitment through Mailings

Colleges compile names for mailing lists from a number of sources. One of their main sources is the Student Search Service, which includes information students voluntarily supply when they take the PSAT/NMSQT or the SAT. Names of prospects with certain characteristics—high math scores or an interest in biology, for instance—are merged on a computer with names assembled in an "inquiry file" created from contacts made with students at college fairs or during visits to high schools by representatives. The inquiry file also includes potential applicants who have sent a letter or postcard requesting information. These "attractive prospects" are sent a packet of materials.

Because mailings are expensive—a mailing of 5,000 packets might produce as few as 400 replies, each one having cost the college around $5 in time and materials—some colleges have learned to increase responses through certain techniques. Individualized salutations for form letters—"Dear Tom, I welcome your interest in our college. . . ."—are used in about half the letters now sent by institutions. In the next few years, probably more colleges will follow the University of Georgia's lead. They will not only greet a potential applicant by his nickname, but include references to his state of residence, his high school, and even his proposed major. Already many schools have switched to using colorful envelopes because studies show that students prefer them. Even the format of a good "search letter" has been established: four to five paragraphs in length, three to four sentences per paragraph, and straightforward language throughout.

Usually included in the information packet are a catalog, various brochures, an application, financial aid information, perhaps a newsletter, and a calendar of events. Less frequently seen are a letter from a department chairperson, the campus newspaper, a letter to parents, or (interestingly) tips on how to choose a college. Also included is a reply card; however, whether or not your child replies makes no difference—he will receive at least two more mailings from that school. You know how it is, once a computer has your name.

From your child's standpoint, most of the information a college sends him will be worthwhile. Encourage him to organize it according to institution. In the long run, this will save time and lead to better-informed decisions.

High School Visits by College Representatives

Besides mailing information packets, another effective way colleges recruit students is by sending admissions representatives to visit high schools. At one time, the role of an admissions person was to review, accept, or deny applications. Lately, however, colleges have been training their representatives to serve as counselors who guide students in their choice of programs. The professional rep will inform students of programs available and alert them to curricular options.

I advise students not to take these visits too lightly. The person they meet might be very influential. Twice I've seen students admitted on the spot because they made a sales pitch to the rep (one of the students was in the bottom sixth of his class). Both students had wisely prepared themselves about their respective college choices: the programs offered, the background of the school, even the reasons the colleges should admit them. And they were told they could count on an offer of admission. It happens.

Ironically, many high schools create impediments that prevent reps from doing their best to inform and counsel students. College representatives are placed out in the hall, shoved under the stairwell, and in one case I know of, stationed in a tool shed at the rear of the cafeteria, with a flashing blue light atop the roof. One representative complained in the *Journal of College Admissions:*

> "Sometimes you may have to sit . . . outside the cafeteria, where you can sniff the fish cakes as you display your wares. In the five minutes between classes . . . you are expected to explain the pros and cons (plus the respective employment opportunities) of the Bachelor-of-Arts-with-Music Concentration versus the Bachelor-of-Music program. Anyone who has frequented a high school at class-changing time—and such an individual is a courageous one—knows that the decibel level is only slightly lower than that of a taxiing Concorde."

If you're really curious, ask your teenager where college representatives meet with students at her high school; ideally, it's in a quiet room with at least half an hour available for students to listen and ask questions. Representatives welcome questions, especially from students who have taken the time to acquaint themselves with the institution beforehand. Here's a list of general questions your child will find worth asking (also see Chapter 4, "How to Make the Right College Choice"):

▶ What does one year cost, room and board included?

▶ Does the college make loans and scholarships available?

▶ Is there a payment plan?

▶ How many courses are in my field?

▶ How large are class sizes for freshmen?

▶ Are remedial or tutorial services available?

▶ Does the school have a job placement office?

▶ How are roommates chosen?

▶ Is there a student health center on campus?

▶ What kind of area is the college located in?

▶ Are there recreational facilities, intramural or collegiate sports?

▶ Is there a Greek system on campus (fraternities and sororities)?

▶ What kinds of religious facilities are located on or near campus?

▶ Are students allowed to have cars on campus?

College Videos

Another way of finding out about colleges is through videos that feature tours of campuses nationwide. With the increasing availability of VCRs, a number of colleges are using video presentations to reach students in other parts of the country.

These presentations, which are generally informative and visually interesting, offer an alternative way for students and their parents to preview campuses that interest them. Check with the guidance office at your child's school, or with your local library, to find out what is available.

College Fairs

If representatives seldom recruit at your child's high school, consider attending a college fair in your area. At one time college fairs were held almost exclusively at high schools or exhibition halls where a couple of hundred representatives could display their brochures and catalogs. With the advent of shopping malls, however, colleges realized they could benefit from recruiting in a well-known location perfectly designed for browsing. Look for mention of upcoming college fairs in the newspaper, and be sure to take a shopping bag so you and your son or daughter can load up on free information. Having on hand a copy of your child's transcript isn't a bad idea either, just in case a representative starts asking about his grade-point average or college prep coursework. (For more information on college fairs, see Chapter 4, "How to Make the Right College Choice.")

Telephone Recruitment

Another recruitment technique that more colleges are turning to is simple and direct—the phone call. Some schools hold phone-a-thons, aptly described by one admissions specialist as a "concentrated multiphone blitz." Whatever name it's given, this type of call is really a sales pitch. From a student's standpoint, it's not particularly helpful because the purpose of the call is *not* informational. In fact, a few colleges have begun employing telemarketing companies to make such calls for them. Many times these callers don't know much of anything about the institution they "represent." In any case answering questions isn't the purpose of recruitment calls. The idea is to get the student to take some action—to visit the campus or perhaps file an application. Here's an example:

Caller: Hello, Bob. This is Dennis King representing the University of _____. We were happy to receive your request for a catalog. Did you get it yet?

Bob: Yes, it came yesterday.

Caller: Good. Well listen, Bob, the reason I'm calling is to invite you to an open house we're having two weeks from tomorrow on the twenty-sixth. Visitors will have a chance to meet students and faculty and tour the campus. There'll also be a cookout for everyone afterwards. Your parents are welcome to attend, too. Do you think you'd like to come?

Bob: Well, sure . . . but I have to ask my dad first.

Caller: OK, fine. Why don't I put you down for now and I'll call back Thursday night with some more details, all right?

Bob: Yeah, OK.

Caller: Great! Hope to meet you and your folks, and remember, I'll call back Thursday. Nice talking to you, Bob. Bye.

Sometimes alumni representatives phone too, but often their information is outdated. You and your child should seek direct contact with a current member of the admissions staff at the college you're considering. Again, ask questions.

But by this point, you and your child will have collected enough information to begin eliminating some schools and looking closely at others.

CHAPTER 7

Testing, Testing: All About Admissions Tests

B ecause I frequently get questions from students and their parents about the role of admissions tests, I'd like to clarify why such tests have been developed, what they are intended to measure, and how they provide objective data that colleges can use—in combination with other information about applicants—to help them reach admission and placement decisions. Before the introduction of standardized admissions tests such as the SAT, colleges had to rely more heavily on subjective judgments, which might put undue emphasis on one aspect of a student while overlooking others. Furthermore, because schools in the United States do not have a uniform curriculum, students' educational experiences and teachers' grading practices vary widely. An admissions test such as the SAT, by being administered under uniform conditions and taking an objective measure of developed verbal and mathematical reasoning abilities, provides a common yardstick against which to measure students' readiness to do college-level work.

No one should assume, of course, that admissions test scores alone will assure a student of getting into a given college. The tests do not measure creativity, motivation, imagination, or even intellectual curiosity. They were never intended for that purpose and college admissions officers are well aware that test scores tell only part of the story about any student's skills and potential for future achievement. That's why it's important to put test scores in perspective. As the College Board, which sponsors the SAT, points out, "grades predict success in college better than the SAT, but the combination of grades and SAT scores helps colleges improve that prediction."

▶ Advice from Admissions Officers

The fact is that there is no "magic number" that guarantees admission, and overemphasizing test scores can lead to unrealistic assumptions. Keep in mind what Susan Murphy, dean of admissions and financial aid at Cornell University, has said: "The SAT is not the most important factor in admissions decisions, even at the most selective institutions. The courses students take in high school and their performance in those courses are most critical."

According to Timm Rinehart, director of admissions at the University of Massachusetts in Amherst, "Students should realize that the SAT is only one of several measures colleges and universities use in admissions. SAT scores are supporting evidence of the high school record, which most of us believe to be the best indicator of college success." In his opinion, the SAT is useful in reaching admissions decisions because it is a reliable, uniform standard for students across the nation.

As Rinehart has pointed out, "Many colleges and universities need such a standard because grades from the nation's 25,000 high schools don't mean the same thing from school to school, and the applicants haven't taken the same courses. By using the SAT to complement the high school record and other factors, colleges can increase the validity of their admissions decisions."

Richard Cashwell, director of undergraduate admissions at the University of North Carolina, Chapel Hill, has noted that "parents and students sometimes think that a 'magic number' on the SAT will guarantee admission or success in college, despite the fact that very few colleges use test scores in a doctrinaire or cut-off fashion."

Cornell's Susan Murphy has said that, contrary to popular belief, there is no formula of grades, test scores, or participation in extracurricular activities that guarantees automatic acceptance by a college. "All these things are important, but a college's decision to admit is not the result of some computerized methodology. It's a thoughtful committee consideration that must take into account a variety of criteria."

Remember, too, that admissions officers look at students in the context of what opportunities were available to them. As Richard Cashwell of the University of North Carolina has said, "The goal is to give rural youngsters from small high schools or minority students from big city schools as good a chance of getting into college as those who go to private schools."

The University of Massachusetts' Timm Rinehart has some words of caution about the hazards of overemphasizing high test scores in the mistaken belief that they guarantee admission to a handful of highly selective colleges. "Parents could lessen some of the pressure on students by realizing that there has to be a match between a student and an institution, and that not all students need to attend the 25 most selective or popular colleges."

As I pointed out earlier, if your child does a realistic job of selecting colleges for which she's academically qualified and that satisfy her priorities, her chances of being admitted to the college of her choice are very good.

▶ About the Tests

The Preliminary Scholastic Aptitude Test/National Merit Scholarship Qualifying Test (PSAT/NMSQT)

The PSAT/NMSQT is an optional test. Most students take it their junior year, although an increasing number of sophomores are signing up for it too—the rationale being that the sooner a person starts preparing for college, the better. Another reason students take the PSAT/NMSQT is that it makes them eligible for a National Merit Scholarship. Black and Hispanic students can also use PSAT/NMSQT results to compete for scholarships offered by the National Achievement Scholarship Program for Outstanding Negro Students and the National Hispanic Scholar Awards Program. Winners in either program are eagerly recruited by colleges and universities.

The PSAT/NMSQT consists of actual SAT questions; it has multiple-choice questions that measure developed verbal and math abilities. Scores from both parts are indicated on a scale of 20-80 (the SAT's scale is 200-800).

Because college admission offices don't depend on the results of the PSAT/NMSQT in their decision-making, taking the exam is good practice for future tests. If your child is disappointed by the results, he can ask his counselor for advice or examine his performance on the test by analyzing his *Report of Student Answers* and consulting the test booklet returned to him—whichever is necessary to improve his performance.

As I mentioned, the PSAT/NMSQT is optional. But the SAT or ACT is either required or preferred by colleges that use test scores to help determine admissibility. Your child can consult a college handbook or the institution's own catalog to find out which exam to take.

The Scholastic Aptitude Test (SAT)

The exam most widely required by colleges is the SAT. Most students take it near the end of their junior year. The verbal part is divided into two sections, each of which includes four types of questions—antonyms, analogies, sentence completion, and reading comprehension. The mathematical portion measures a student's ability to solve problems involving arithmetic reasoning, algebra, and geometry. In fact, any student who has had two years of high school math—one of geometry and one of algebra—should be adequately prepared for the math portion of the SAT.

One thing to remember about the SAT is that there's a guessing penalty: test takers lose a fraction of a point for each wrong answer. In *Taking the SAT,* which is the official guide to the Scholastic Aptitude Test, the College Board says that if the student knows that one or more answers to a question are definitely wrong, it's generally a good idea to guess from the remaining choices. But because of the penalty for incorrect answers, random guessing isn't likely to increase a student's score.

The American College Test (ACT)

The ACT is a different animal in several ways. Because of its academic content, most students delay taking it until fall of their senior year. The exam has four sections: English, math, social studies, and natural science. Each is scored on a scale of 1-36 with a composite given for the entire exam, and unlike the SAT, there's no penalty for wrong answers. So if your child sees that time is running out to finish the tests, she should "take ACTion" and fill in the rest of those dots as quickly as she can.

The English usage portion of the ACT emphasizes clear and effective expression rather than recall of grammar rules. The mathematics usage test measures mathematical reasoning ability by presenting the kinds of problems encountered in math courses. The social studies reading test is divided into two parts. The first part asks questions about four passages taken from social studies material (political science, geography, history, and economics). The second is a series of multiple-choice questions based on general information taught in social studies courses. The last section of the exam is the natural science reading test, which examines whether the student can analyze, interpret, and apply information taken from scientific data, such as reports of experiments. This portion uses science vocabulary.

Additional Tests

Sometimes colleges and universities require additional exams for the purpose of placement in freshman courses. Many colleges require three College Board Achievement Tests in specific content areas, such as biology, English, or math. Each test lasts an hour, and the college will always indicate which tests it requires.

Also, many colleges require applicants whose native language is other than English to submit scores from the Test of English as a Foreign Language (TOEFL). The admissions office can answer questions about this.

Taking Examinations for College Credit

Finally, several examinations offer high school students the opportunity to earn college credit. In Chapter 3, I described one such option, Advanced Placement Examinations. An alternate route is the College-Level Examination Program (CLEP). More than 1,700 colleges offer credit through CLEP; even so, if your child knows which colleges he plans to apply to, it's a good idea to find out whether they participate in the program.

CLEP tests are administered throughout the year at more than 1,000 test centers throughout the country. Your child should ask for a list of centers in the high school guidance office. There are two kinds of CLEP tests: General Examinations cover English, composition, humanities, mathematics, natural science, and social science; Subject Examinations are available in 30 different areas. Both types are based on the content covered in college courses. They measure factual knowledge, as well as the ability to see relationships and apply basic principles. Under certain conditions, the tests may be taken a second time in a 12-month period. The deadline for sending special requests and registration forms is four weeks before each upcoming test date (see Glossary).

Preparing for Admissions Tests

There are differences of opinion on the subject of special preparation for admissions tests such as the SAT. However, many educators believe that short-term drill and cramming are not very effective but that longer term preparation that emphasizes studying widely in academic subject areas and reading extensively can help students increase their scores.

Test sponsors provide all test registrants with a free booklet that contains guidelines on how to prepare for the test. The College Board's *Taking the SAT,* for example, includes test-taking strategies; a review of skills, concepts, and question types; a full sample test with answers; scoring instructions; and an answer sheet. The Board's advice to students is to familiarize themselves with the organization of the test, the types of questions that will appear on it, and what will be expected of them on the test day, all of which can be done by following the steps outlined below:

▶ Read the test booklet all the way through to become familiar with all aspects of the test, noting any parts that seem important or confusing so that they can be given special attention.

▶ Study the sample questions and explanations to get a good idea of the kinds of questions on the test. Students are generally more at ease on the day of the actual test if they know beforehand what to expect.

▶ Study and understand the test directions so that less time will have to be spent reading and figuring them out on the test day, leaving more time for answering the questions.

▶ Take the sample test under conditions as close to the actual ones as possible. In other words, the test should be taken at a cleared desk or table; it should be completed in one sitting within the time limitations specified for each section.

What About Coaching Courses?

On the subject of coaching, the College Board strongly recommends that students carefully consider what they can do in their regular schoolwork, independently in their leisure time, or working with fellow students or adults to prepare for admissions tests without distracting from other things that are important to their education and college aims. If you and your youngster are convinced that special preparation outside regular classroom activities will make a difference, first find out what your child's school has to offer before deciding to pay for a course. If nothing is available, be sure to get satisfactory answers to the following key questions before your child enrolls in a coaching course.

What's the philosophy behind the course? A valuable course includes practice questions with follow-up explanations of why some answers are wrong.

What's the extent of the course? A worthwhile course should be spread over a reasonable length of time; forget about weekend "crash courses." There should be a substantial number of classroom hours involved. And stay away from outfits that just sell your child a do-it-yourself workbook—he can buy cheaper ones at any major bookstore.

How much will it cost? Ask the price of books, tapes, lectures, all of it. Some courses offer guarantees: a refund if your child doesn't reach a goal, or maybe a discount if she repeats the course.

Finally, if you know someone who's been through the course, encourage your child to get his opinion.

Don't automatically assume that your adolescent can't enroll in a coaching course because of money constraints. A few don't insist on cash up front and offer the option of deferred payment plans. Ask about scholarships, too. In your own community, you might try enlisting the help of the PTSA, the clergy, or local civic groups. At least one benefit you can count on is that your child will be able to mention these efforts on his college applications. And believe me, admissions personnel look favorably on this kind of gumption.

Registering for the Exams

To register for the SAT or ACT, your child must pick up a packet of materials in the high school guidance office. Inside the packet will be a registration form and instructions. Registration deadlines are five to six weeks before the test date. As the instructions will explain, send the fee directly to the test company. About a week before the exam, your son or daughter will receive an admission ticket *that must be taken to the test center on the test date.*

I advise students to get a good night's sleep on the eve of the exam, and to get up in plenty of time to avoid rushing. They should have a good breakfast and dress in easily removable layers of clothing in case the room is too hot. In addition to the admission ticket, they will also need some positive form of identification, two No. 2 pencils, and a watch. After they arrive, they should sit away from friends, relax, and just get comfortable before the exam begins.

Releasing Test Scores to Colleges

When registering for the SAT or ACT, your child will have the opportunity to make information about herself available to colleges across the country just by checking a box on the registration form. The way these services work is this. Let's say, for example, that a college is looking for students with strong math scores who are planning to major in engineering. The college's admissions office can purchase a computer tape of the names and addresses of examinees who have these characteristics, and then generate a specialized mailing list. Scholarship and governmental agencies use the service the same way. Over 1,000 colleges purchase the College Board's Student Search Service, and more than a million students participate each year. In a recent survey of 3,000 students, more than half of the respondents termed the service "very valuable" because of the college brochures and applications they received. Not surprisingly, many students also receive materials from institutions that they couldn't care less about.

Whether or not your child participates in the Student Search Service, test score reports should be sent directly to the colleges from the testing agencies, never from the applicant herself. Test registration forms provide space in which your child can list the colleges that she has chosen to receive her scores. Then again, some students don't list any colleges the first time they take the exam. They wait until they have received their scores and then decide whether they're satisfied with the results. If so, they can request additional score reports, for an additional fee, and have the results forwarded to particular colleges. This strategy seems to lessen the pressure on students considerably, and I often recommend it to young people who seem to dread taking the exams.

Dealing with Disappointment

Many times every school year students come to see me because they are unhappy with their scores. More often than not, their disappointment is based on a false premise: namely, that their score(s) *should* have been higher. Here's a typical conversation:

Student: "Mr. Shields, I can't believe what I got on the SAT. I thought I was going to do better."

Shields: "What'd you get?"

Student: "540 on the verbal and 620 on math."

Shields: "Can I ask your grade-point average?"

Student: "About 3.0."

Shields: "Where are you in your class?"

Student: "Upper quarter."

Shields: "Your score is right about on the money."

The standardized test score is supposed to reflect a student's grades. If it's way above his grades, a college is going to assume he hasn't been working to capacity in class. If, on the other hand, the score is way below, most colleges will assume that the applicant had a bad day or was feeling nervous.

"But wait a minute," students and parents will protest. "It says right here in the college's own catalog that the admissions office wants, on the SAT, for example, a 550 math and a 525 verbal. That doesn't hint at any flexibility!"

The test figures in college handbooks and catalogs are usually median scores; that is, 50 percent of applicants score above them, and 50 percent score below. Surveys have shown that most colleges will seriously consider candidates who score 2 points on either side of the stated ACT figure, and 100 points on either side of the SAT figure.

Nevertheless, if your child is unhappy with the scores, she has options. If she suspects that there's been a mistake, she can request that the test be rescored by hand for a small additional fee. Should your child want to repeat a test, and the test publisher makes copies of questions and answers available, your child may wish to request them and review her strengths and weaknesses.

A second test score, I must emphasize, is not likely to be significantly higher than the first and may, in fact, be lower. According to the College Board, "When students take tests more than once they usually find that their scores change. This change may be due to academic growth, to practice, or to both. For those students whose scores change when they repeat the test, about 60 percent have a score increase, while about 40 percent have a score decrease."

If standardized tests have always been a problem for your adolescent, rather than taking a particular exam over (and over), she should mention this difficulty on the college application or offer an explanation in a cover letter.

CHAPTER 8

A Word about Special Students: Athletes, Minorities, and the Disabled

For some applicants, the chance for success at college depends more than for most students on how thoroughly they research their choices before they apply. The "fit" between these special students and their college tends to be more important for them than it is for most applicants. A student athlete, for instance, can't be satisfied with knowing only that his top choice has a good team. He must also ask certain additional questions: What happens if I don't play after my freshman year? Will tutoring or counseling be available if I fall behind in my studies?

Likewise, a minority applicant must press for answers to her concerns: If I'm accepted under a special admissions program, what can I expect in the way of academic advising and remedial services?

And for a disabled student, a lot will depend on whether his favorite choices have services and facilities that meet his special needs.

In this chapter we will look at the extra dimensions that these categories of students—athletes, minorities, and the disabled— add to their college search because of special circumstances.

College Bound Athletes

When a high school athlete daydreams about playing sports at college, does he see himself sitting humbly on the bench waiting for the coach to send him in? Probably not. He sees himself acknowledging the cheers of the fans, granting an interview in the locker room after the game, and weighing the merits of an attractive offer to "go professional." In short, he shares the same fantasy thousands of other young men and women have: college will be his springboard to the big leagues and then his fortune will be assured.

Unfortunately, the facts don't support this notion at all. These are the facts:

▶ Only 2 out of every 100 college basketball players make it to the pros.

▶ The professionals in any major sport are usually drawn from big institutions, which are treasure troves of first-rate athletes playing on outstanding teams.

▶ The average pro football career lasts only three years.

These harsh realities affirm that the college-bound athlete and his parents must plan ahead for the inevitable time when the cheering stops. Careers in sports can end abruptly if a starting spot evaporates after only one year, or if a player's interest or athletic abilities suddenly wane. When your child talks to recruiters and coaches, encourage him to keep his priorities in order: college first, sports second. Emphasize, as is said in business, the long-term advantage over the short-term gain.

Prerecruitment Planning

Before recruiters appear on the scene, try to get a realistic assessment of your teenager's potential by making an appointment with his or her high school coach. If you want the coach to be as candid as possible, make the appointment for yourself only. Ask him to compare your son's or daughter's abilities with those of other college-bound athletes. Where, in the coach's opinion, would your child fare best: in the sports program of a small, medium or large institution? Does the coach have any college-level contacts that he'd be willing to use? Would he write your child a recommendation? Whatever his answers, get a second opinion from another coach or perhaps from the school principal. Don't let your child shape his plans around the personal feelings, positive or negative, of only one individual.

The second prerecruitment step is this: learn all you can about the rules governing recruitment. Depending on which level of competition your child is considering, his or her relationship with a recruiter must abide by rules established by the National

Collegiate Athletic Association (NCAA), and the National Junior College Athletic Association (NJCAA). Violating any of the regulations might result in your son or daughter being barred from competition, or might cause the college itself to be placed on probation. An excellent book to have on hand, one that deals not only with recruitment but with pressures and choices collegiate players must face, is *The Athlete's Game Plan for College and Career* by Stephen and Howard Figler, published by Peterson's Guides, Princeton, NJ, 1985. You can also write to the following associations for information:

> National Collegiate Athletic Association (NCAA)
> P.O. Box 1906
> Mission, KS 66222

> National Association for Intercollegiate Athletics (NAIA)
> 1221 Baltimore Avenue
> Kansas City, MO 64105

> National Junior College Athletic Association (NJCAA)
> P.O. Box 1586
> Hutchinson, KS 67504

> California Association of Community Colleges (CACC)
> 2017 O Street
> Sacramento, CA 95814

The Athlete's Resume

In helping your college-bound athlete make plans, keep in mind that recruitment is not the only route to collegiate sports. It might be that your child's coach doesn't have any "ins" at colleges, or perhaps the colleges you're looking at don't recruit in your son's or daughter's sport. An alternative is to work with your child on a resume of his or her athletic accomplishments and send it to targeted colleges and universities. You can obtain the names and addresses of specific coaches you wish to reach by referring to *Callahan's College Guide to Athletics and Academics in America* by Timothy R. Callahan, published by Harper & Row Publishers, NY (updated annually).

▶ Below is an example of one young man's resume:

JEFF JONES

1993 Crown Drive	Born 12/2/68
Waltham, Iowa 51607	6'0"
(817) 555-1212	175 lbs.

EDUCATION

Waltham Public High School, grades 9-12. Enrollment: 2,400. Conference: Northeast Iowa Athletic, Division I. Address: 1203 Main Street, Waltham, Iowa 51607.

Chester Conklin Junior High School (public), grades 7-8. Enrollment: 425. Conference: none. Address: 487 Blackhawk Drive, Waltham, Iowa 51607.

EDUCATIONAL BACKGROUND

Maintained a B average during junior high and high school
ACT 21 SAT 500 V 530 M
Top one-third of class

EXTRACURRICULAR ACTIVITIES

Key Club during grades 10, 11, 12
Varsity Men's Club during grades 11, 12
Speech team (radio broadcasting) during grades 10, 11

COMMUNITY SERVICE & WORK EXPERIENCES

Stock clerk at Munch Pharmacy, 511 S. Broad Street, Waltham, Iowa 51607, for three years part-time
Political volunteer for State Representative Bill Magnum
Waltham Community Church Youth Organization

ATHLETIC BACKGROUND

Golf

Played three years on State Golf Team (team finished 2nd in state, 1986)
Golf medalist (1985, 1986)

Varsity (1985, 1986)
Attended Les Arnstein's Summer Golf Camp (1985)
Highest Individual Points (1986)
Des Moines Register "Athlete of the Week" (Oct., 1985)
Golf Digest Most Improved Junior Golfer (1985)

Gymnastics

Competed for three years (team finished 3rd in state, 1986)
1st Place all-conference floor event, sophomore year
Varsity (1985, 1986)
2nd Place all-conference on parallel bars (1986)
4th Place in sectionals on parallel bars (1986)
13th in state on parallel bars (1986)

ATHLETIC GOALS

I plan to attend a college or university where I can compete in golf at the Division I level.

REFERENCES

Bob Bohl, head golf coach, Waltham High School, 584–1047
Mark Evans, head gymnastics coach, Waltham High School, 584-1053
Les Arnstein, golf camp coordinator, Wheatley, Iowa, 643-3284

▶ Below is a sample letter to accompany Jeff's resume:

Stuart Mills
Head Golf Coach
State University
Harbor, Arkansas 18723

Dear Coach Mills:
I am a senior at Waltham High School in Waltham, Iowa, and am interested in playing golf at State University. Enclosed is my resume.
Please send me information about your golf program, including information on scholarships for players. Thank you.

Sincerely,

Tips for the Recruited Athlete

Let's say the resume produces a few phone calls from coaches, or perhaps your teenager is approached by a recruiter via some other route. What should your child do? What questions should he ask? Here are 10 general tips about recruiting for you to share with your young athlete:

Establish the recruiter's relationship to the school. Is he the head coach, the assistant coach, an alumnus, or an admissions representative? Assurances carry different weights depending on their sources.

Keep your education foremost in your mind. A good recruiter is as informed about academic programs as an admissions officer. Fire away with specific questions about majors and courses in your field.

Ask at which level your sport competes. NCAA Division I schools offer athletic scholarships; some Division II schools do not; no Division III schools do as a matter of policy.

Ask for the details about athletic scholarships—any strings? Typically, athletic scholarships (or grants as they're sometimes called) are for one year, renewable at the coach's discretion. If you get benched, must you start paying your own way from then on?

Ask how many athletes were kept on scholarship after their eligibility had expired. Because of heavy demands on their time, some college athletes take five years to graduate. By their final year they're usually ineligible to play.

Ask whether tutoring or counseling will be available. Beware of remarks like, "Don't worry—we haven't lost a player yet due to academics," which could imply that your education will be allowed to suffer before the welfare of the team will.

Ask what will happen if you're placed on academic probation. Do you lose part of your benefits? All of them?

Make an appointment to talk to the coach in your sport. Ask what he expects from his players: time commitment, behavior, appearance, etc. Decide whether you can work with him.

Talk to your potential teammates. What have their experiences been like? What advice would they give someone like yourself?

If your college-bound athlete keeps these 10 points in mind, he will go a long way toward avoiding misunderstandings with the college he comes to represent.

Eligibility Requirements

Speaking of misunderstandings, one of the vaguest areas confronting high school athletes is player eligibility. Whereas most nonathletes seeking admission have to meet fairly clear-cut criteria—grade-point average, rank in class, test scores, etc. —athletes sometimes find themselves in an additional, subtler game with "flexible" rules.

For Division I athletes, the NCAA has tried to make eligibility requirements simple and nonnegotiable. An applicant who plans to compete must have received high school credit and maintained at least a 2.0 (C average) in 11 college prep courses. The minimum number of courses in each subject area is:

▶ three English

▶ two mathematics

▶ two social sciences

▶ two (or one laboratory course if it's available at the high school) natural or physical sciences

Finally, the Division I applicant must also have scored at least a 700 composite on the Scholastic Aptitude Test (SAT) or at minimum a 15 on the American College Test (ACT).

At other levels of collegiate competition, however, requirements concerning not only eligibility but also admission are not nearly as definite. If your child ends up on an admissions waiting list or seems to be a marginal candidate, he will almost certainly be admitted if the admissions office knows that one of the coaches wants him. Minority athletes, in particular, tend to be admitted to institutions at which they might not otherwise be accepted, because colleges have learned two things: first, admitting minority athletes is one way to achieve racial diversity, and second, strong athletic programs are money producers. The danger is that special admissions programs with assigned tutors or mandatory study halls are sometimes used to disguise a second-rate education. You and your young athlete can educate yourselves about potential abuses by requesting a free copy of *Your Rights and Responsibilities as a Student Athlete in Higher Education* from:

> The National Association of Student Personnel
> Administrators
> P.O. Box 21265
> Columbus, OH 43221

Your child's best strategy to avoid being recruited out of his academic league is to consider only those schools he would be admitted to regardless of his athletic talents. That way he will avoid letting himself in for an education that is either too challenging or less than adequate.

Minority Students

As I was researching this book, the alumni development office of my college alma mater called one evening asking for a donation. By coincidence, I had just read an article about the low enrollment figures for minorities at that university, so I said that I would contribute but added, half-jokingly, "Tell the Dean to get those minority figures up." A few days later I received a long, sincere letter from an associate dean describing what the university was doing to attract and retain minority students.

Colleges and universities do recognize that a disproportionately low number of minority students go on to college. Just look at the lopsided figures: for every 100 white Americans who enter the first grade, 24 will graduate from college; for every 100 blacks, 8 will; for every 100 Hispanic-Americans, 5 will. As you can imagine, colleges are eager to increase their minority enrollments. Nevertheless, minority students and their parents should be cautious, and not let themselves become the victims of overzealous recruiting.

Recruitment of Minority Students

At the outset, minority students are contacted through the same channels used to recruit other college-bound students. Colleges that require more than a high school diploma—selective colleges, they're called—try to recruit minority students who come to their attention through the National Merit Scholarship and the National

Achievement Scholarship Program for Outstanding Negro Students. Other minority students are recruited through contacts with school counselors, administrators, and community leaders and by representatives at career and college fairs.

Cultural Diversity

Schools that deserve a second look from minority applicants and their families offer cultural diversity and certain kinds of special programs.

Where there is little cultural diversity, certain accepted ways of thinking and acting usually prevail. Most of the students may belong to the same social class, share many of the same viewpoints, and come from a similar religious background. Lack of cultural diversity can breed intolerance, plain and simple.

On the other hand, a campus that is culturally diverse welcomes differences among people. Its college catalog will list clubs and organizations representing a range of political, social, and ethnic identities. Included might be a club for students who are politically liberal, and one for those who are not. You and your son or daughter should also look for groups like the Hispanic Students Union or such events as an annual walkathon for Israel as evidence that the campus is not culturally dominated by one type of student.

Special Programs for Minorities

Special programs of value to minority students include tutoring and remedial services, counseling services staffed by other minority students, and financial aid services that help students over short-term money crises.

Generally, private colleges have a better track record than public schools for retaining minority students by means of well-developed programs like these. However, the only way to verify that a particular school has these kinds of services is to visit the campus. Don't depend on a representative's word; don't depend on an alumnus who says, "I'm not sure how many minority students we have, but there are probably a lot, so we should have the kinds of programs you're asking about." See for yourself.

Many colleges have developed a special admissions program for educationally and socioeconomically disadvantaged students, a high percentage of whom are also minority students. These applications are usually reviewed with great care, and factors other than an applicant's high school record and test scores are weighed. For example, the performance of already-enrolled minority students who had similar grades in high school is used as a basis for prediction. The reviewer may also look at the candidate's family background. Is "going to college" a new experience for this family? In other words, does the candidate have an idea of what to expect? Finally, recommendations from teachers, counselors, and community members are read thoroughly. Overall, the applicant's file should indicate that she has a goal in mind and is willing to work to achieve it—the two most important factors in making a special admissions decision. The applicant's high school may have been substandard, or her preparation may have been inadequate, but these shortcomings can be overlooked in favor of qualities that say, "This person has the potential we're looking for."

Merely getting into college, however, will not automatically put your child on Easy Street. Before signing up for first-semester classes, she should see an academic advisor and get a feel for the size of the challenge ahead. Perhaps she will be advised to take a study skills class or to carry a light academic load for the first year until she's confident about her abilities.

For future reference, the following three situations sometimes prevent minority students from reaching their full potential at college. All three concern stereotyping.

Pitfalls to Avoid

First, don't let your son or daughter be steered into a major because of a generalization someone makes about the child's ethnic or racial background. Not all Orientals are good at math and science; therefore, not all of them should be counseled into majoring in these areas. Likewise, not all black students should tackle social service careers because that's where they're "needed."

A second problem involving stereotyping can develop when too little is expected of minority students. Some college instructors, for whatever reasons, grade minority students on a separate, less rigorous scale. This kind of double standard convinces many minority students that they're getting a second-rate education— and they're right. If this problem crops up in one of your child's classes, he should explain the situation to the Dean of Academic Advising or the department chairperson.

Finally, there's a tendency among many minority students, when arriving at college, to immediately seek out others like themselves. Initially, this strategy may provide support and comfort, but in the long run it can prove limiting. Part of your

child's college experience—indeed, part of her college education—
should include meeting people different from herself. Encourage
your child to expand his world beyond the doors of the black
fraternity house or the all-night meetings of the Committee on
Hispanic Concerns. He will discover that there is an exciting
education to be had in the coffee houses and on the intramural
playing fields of college, as well. These are places where students talk, have fun, exchange ideas, and sometimes forge friendships that last a lifetime.

Physically Impaired and Learning Disabled Students

Services for disabled students have greatly increased over the
last 10 years as a result of efforts by the federal government and
by colleges themselves. Many colleges and universities have
standing committees that evaluate and improve on-campus facilities and services for these students. Also, preadmission interviews,
programs with special options, and increased social activities for
impaired students in particular have become common features on
many campuses.

Federal Regulations

According to federal regulations, a disabled person is someone
with a physical or mental impairment that substantially limits
one or more major life activities, someone who has a record of
such impairment or is regarded as having such an impairment.
Disabling conditions include a physiological disorder or condition, a cosmetic disfigurement, or an anatomical loss affecting a
body system. Life activities impaired as the result of a disability
include caring for one's physical needs, performing manual tasks,
walking, seeing, hearing, breathing, speaking, learning, and
working. Under this definition come students who are considered
learning disabled.

   If your child has a disability, the key piece of legislation
regulating the relationship between her and a college is the
Rehabilitation Act of 1973, which is essentially a civil rights law.
Section 504 of the act provides that "no otherwise qualified
handicapped individual . . . shall solely by reason of his handicap,
be excluded from the participation in, be denied the benefits of,
or be subjected to discrimination under any program or activity
receiving federal financial assistance."

   This prohibition against discrimination applies not only to
admissions, but also to recruitment, publications, admissions tests,

financial aid, and orientation activities. In addition, your child may not be denied the use of such aids as a tape recorder or guide dog. If necessary, the college must provide auxiliary aids, such as interpreters or taped texts.

That's a summary of conditions by which colleges and universities are required to abide. They are exempt, however, from the following: Colleges do not have to provide attendants, individual prescription devices, people who will read materials for personal use or study, or other devices or services of a personal nature. Even more important, Section 504 does not require an institution to *lower or make major changes in its standards to accommodate a handicapped person.* This means that it falls to you and your son or daughter to evaluate the services and facilities of colleges in which you are interested. After your child has been accepted, he must take the institution pretty much as it is.

Choice of College

If your child is learning disabled, a good place to start looking for the right institution is *Colleges with Programs for Learning Disabled Students* (Peterson's Guides, Princeton, NJ, 1988). This book profiles 279 four-year colleges in the United States that offer programs for students with learning disabilities. In the book's introduction, the authors tell how to recognize learning disabilities, deal with them, and choose the correct college program for a learning-disabled student.

If your physically impaired or learning disabled child does not need a comprehensive program but does need some special services, write for the catalogs of the individual schools that interest you and check to see what services are provided. Some colleges will send pamphlets and brochures about services and facilities for the disabled if requested.

As you might expect, visiting a school is crucial if your child is disabled. Call the admissions office and ask for a tour of the campus. Also, request a personal interview for your child and inquire about financial aid reserved specifically for disabled students. Ask whether there are organizations of disabled persons on campus, and how you can get in contact with them. Advice from disabled students may be very helpful.

Tips for the Disabled Student

Here are some tips for physically handicapped students once they are enrolled.

▶ Never register for a class without knowing how you can get there.

▶ Always make arrangements with professors beforehand if special conditions are necessary to your class participation.

▶ Resist being counseled to prepare for traditional social service positions for the disabled if that kind of work isn't appealing to you.

▶ Finally, never leave anything until the last minute.

Whether your child is an athlete, a minority student, disabled, or a prospective student without special needs, if she has narrowed her choices down to several institutions, she is now ready to take action toward achieving her goal. That next major step, applying to colleges, is the subject of the following chapter.

CHAPTER 9

Applications That Open Doors

Each year, 2.5 million American high school students apply to more than 3,000 colleges and universities. Out of this annual pool of applicants, the majority receive acceptances from the institution that was their first choice. Moreover, 92 percent of those who apply to two or more colleges are accepted by at least two.

Surprised? In regard to public institutions, high incidence of candidate rejection is largely a myth. Practically anyone who wants to go to college can be admitted someplace. Even a private, selective school must offer approximately 5,000 acceptances to enroll a class of 1,500, because so many applicants have opportunities to go elsewhere. Only at about 15 percent of all colleges and universities is the competition so intense that acceptance is really touch-and-go.

Regardless, most people interpret acceptance by a college as a prize or a seal of approval that establishes a person's worth; consequently, many books and articles about the college selection process play on the theme of the mythological "admissions game." Strategies are offered that supposedly "psych out" interviewers; examples are given on how to describe ordinary experiences on a college application so that they appear to be important and creative endeavors.

Handled appropriately, though, applying to college is not some kind of game. The process should reveal to a young person something about his goals. The experience should introduce him to adult responsibilities such as providing factual information about himself, meeting deadlines, and making the kinds of decisions that others have previously made *for* him.

On a family level, applying to college signifies that the teen-ager is preparing to grow into new roles, ones that will probably provide more independence. As more of the young person's time is spent away from the watchful eye of Mom and Dad, personal choices will have to be made without benefit of their advice. Sometimes this impending separation causes reenactments of old childhood struggles. Parents may attempt to reassert control by badgering their children about application deadlines, and the children counter that they resent being pushed around by their parents. Not only is applying to college often seen as a game, but in many households it must resemble a tug-of-war.

Some parents respond to the application process by throwing up their hands and letting their teenager sink or swim. Others charge in and take over the paperwork, implying that the child isn't up to the effort that college requires (if so, then why let him attend?). As you can imagine, neither approach inspires confi-dence in a child, and that's exactly what she needs as she faces one of the first major opportunities of her life.

As the guidelines of the National Association of College Admis-sion Counselors state, when you're applying to college you have the responsibility:

▶ To be aware of the policies (deadlines, restrictions, etc.) regarding admissions and financial aid of colleges and universities of your choice.

▶ To complete and submit required material to colleges and universities.

▶ To meet all application deadlines.

▶ To follow college application procedures of your high school.

▶ To notify the colleges and universities which have offered you admission of your acceptance or rejection of their offer as soon as you have heard from all to which you have applied, or by May 1, whichever is earlier.

The best way to make the experience of applying to college one that will contribute to your child's development is to emphasize that by being organized she can handle nearly all of the steps herself. The process is a fitting rehearsal for tasks that adults routinely do: apply for loans, file tax returns, conduct a job hunt, to name a few. Your young adult *can* and *should* learn to do this kind of work on her own.

Applying to a Range of Institutions

The first order of business is deciding how many applications to submit. I recommend that your child apply to at least four institutions: one that will definitely admit him, two that he feels fairly certain about, and one that he will be accepted by if there are such things as miracles. The reason for hedging his bet is simple: if he takes aim only at a couple of "easy" institutions, he will wonder later whether he underestimated his chances. On the other hand, if he applies only to "long shots" (as one of my counselees unfortunately did) he might be denied by all of them (as she was). Odds are that if your child spreads his applications over a range of colleges with increasingly selective admissions standards, he'll probably be accepted by more than one—and, who knows, perhaps by the most selective of all.

Keeping Track of the Paperwork

It will be critical that your child keep records. Each of the "powers that be" connected with college admissions—testing companies, financial aid administrators, and admissions offices themselves—has deadlines that your child cannot afford to miss. In addition, colleges and universities practice a variety of admissions policies—each with its own timetable: Rolling admissions, Deferred admission, Early Admission, Early Decision, Early Evaluation, and Early Action (see Glossary).

Another good reason for keeping records is that not all colleges will require the same information from your child. Generally, a high school transcript is the most commonly requested credential. Next, approximately 70 percent of all colleges require ACT or SAT test scores. When it comes to Achievement Tests, letters of recommendation, and personal interviews, private colleges are much more likely to require these than public institutions.

The simplest way for your child to keep track of the paperwork is to use file folders: one for test score reports, one for each college being applied to, one for financial aid information, and so on. On the outside of the college folders she should record dates: when applications were sent, when recommendations were requested from teachers and counselors, and when transcripts were mailed from school. Recording the "what, when, and where" for each piece of correspondence—and its outcome—can help the application process to proceed smoothly.

Incidentally, an aspect of being organized that young people often overlook has to do with phone conversations related to admissions. Usually applicants are unprepared with pen and paper to take down dates, names, addresses and other pieces of useful information. Urge your son or daughter to jot down notes while talking, so that both of you are later spared scenes like this:

You: "Well, what did he say?"

Child: "He said I had to get it in soon."

You: "Soon? When's 'soon'? Tomorrow? Next week? When?"

Child: "I don't know . . . *soon.*"

Completing the Application

Now that your child has decided which schools he will apply to and has set up an organized record keeping system, he can begin filing applications.

First, he'll need an application from each institution he's considering. Colleges will usually send an application when a catalog is requested. (If your child sends an application before requesting a current information packet, for some reason, he should check to make sure it's current.)

Many young people are tempted to tackle the first few applications that arrive and muddle through them one at a time. This is not the best approach. Instead, your child should do two things before she even fills in her name. First, it's a good idea to make a photocopy of each blank application as a practice copy. When all the information is correctly entered, and the personal essay has gone through its final draft, then your child can type on the original. Second, she should begin work on the applications *in order of their deadlines.* Even the neatest, most sincere application won't move the heart of an admissions director if it's late in arriving.

Listing Awards and Achievements

Some young people are intimidated by the length of many applications; one rough spot in particular is the space labeled "awards, honors, and distinctions." Rather than trying to recall examples of these from memory, I suggest your teenager do the following: assemble scrapbooks, diaries, certificates, diplomas, ribbons, medals, letters of appreciation, and anything else of this sort she has saved over the years. To this she should add a list of significant experiences she's had: vacations, camps, competitions, recitals, and performances. If she's still short on "awards, honors, and distinctions," she can compile a list labeled "Twenty Things of Which I'm Proud." She should give a one-sentence description of each experience or event, and then explain why she's proud of it. Your child should also pick up a high school coursebook so that she can refer to courses by their exact titles, and describe their content if necessary. Together, these things will make up a stockpile of dates, experiences, and important moments that will make those yawning white spaces on the application much less intimidating.

Describing Extracurricular Involvement

Another place on the application that often trips up students is the section where they are asked to list their extracurricular activities in high school. Your child, like most young people, will probably want to appear a "well-rounded student"; he'll be tempted to list himself as a member of the school's Key Club, for example, even if he only helped out on one Pancake Day during his sophomore year. Actually, including this kind of marginal participation will work against him. As we discussed in Chapter 3, colleges and universities would rather see that he participated in a couple of activities over a period of a year or more than that he flirted with a dozen organizations for less than a semester each. Having earned a spot as class president by junior year or having served as news editor on the school paper are genuine achievements; having dabbled in a number of other things is not. On the whole, then, your child is certain to make a better impression by being selective about the activities he lists.

In the same vein, students tend to greatly overstate the amount of time they spend on homework or employment, which produces unlikely totals. An associate director of admissions once reviewed an application on which the candidate said she worked 30 hours a week, spent an average of 3 to 4 hours a night on homework, and still managed to do volunteer work 15 hours a week. His comment was, "Evidently this girl has given up sleeping." Caution your child to give a realistic description of how she spends her time.

So much for supplying routine information. Now let's talk about the most demanding requirement of all: the personal essay part of the application.

Writing a Personal Essay

Not all colleges require a personal essay. Those that do often have their own preferred topics. Some will try to get a glimpse of your child's intellectual interests by posing a question like this: Suppose you are going to be stranded on a deserted island and you can take only three books with you. Which ones would you take, and why?

Others describe situations that require the applicant to philosophize. Here's one: Imagine that you are an astronaut stranded on Mars (perhaps applications pose so many "stranded" dilemmas because nervous applicants can easily identify with them). You can't return by rocket, but you have a machine that will transmit an identical reproduction of you to Earth. Every molecule of you will be in place as it is. In the process, however, you will be destroyed. The question is, will the copy received on Earth be you, or will you have ceased to exist?

Some colleges may give your child a choice among several different topics, although he would probably like to respond by writing "None of the above." And then there are essay topics that look deceptively simple but that can be the most challenging of all. Here's an example: Please tell us about yourself. Beneath this is an entirely blank page, as cold and white as a stretch of Arctic landscape.

Whatever the topic, a good personal essay is important not so much for its content but because it puts the writer in perspective. A personal essay that impresses an admissions reviewer succeeds at doing two things. First, it proves that the applicant can write effectively. And second, it gives some insight into the person behind the facts. Other parts of the application will ask when your child was born or where he went to school, but the personal essay is an opportunity for your child to introduce characteristics or interests that will put him in the best possible light. When I give a student pointers on personal essay writing, I encourage him to use the following six keys to create a memorable image of himself on paper.

Key 1: *Put yourself in perspective.*
Contrast yourself against a background so that the reader can get an idea of your individuality. Here's an example:

> If you saw me sitting near you on the commuter train
> that runs through my neighborhood, you'd probably think,
> Now there's a real city kid—a little tough looking, ignor-
> ing everyone else, and carrying a radio. But if you looked

closer, you'd see that I was reading. And what I like to
read is just about anything that has to do with history:
19th-century novels, biographies of famous people, you
name it.

Doesn't this create a picture of someone you can imagine, and not
just a retelling of facts that would appear elsewhere on the
application?

Key 2: *Use plain, simple English.*
In the example above, you can hear the person speaking.
It's as though he were talking to you in person. No one really
goes around sounding like an encyclopedia, although you
may be tempted to write like that in a personal essay
because you think it will impress the reader. Don't believe
it. What British writer Virginia Woolf once remarked is true:
"Good writing reads like good conversation." Sound like yourself on paper, and drop any phrase or paragraph that seems
contrived.

Key 3: *Use a special focus or angle to tie the essay together.*
If you decide to describe an experience, it should illustrate
some important aspect of yourself. For example, perhaps
you took a trip to a foreign country, and what you heard and
saw made you rethink some of your values. To take another
approach, you might retell an experience as a way of communicating ideas that are important to you. Let's say you
spent a summer working as a counselor at a camp for small
children. Instead of describing everything that happened,
you could focus on one incident as a way of expressing your
thoughts about responsibility, maturity, or education.

Key 4: *Link your goals with how you can contribute to the
college.* "I want" is one of the most common phrases seen
in applications essays: I want to enjoy what the university
has to offer; I want to study in your excellent physics department; I want to expand my thinking, my outlook, and so on.
But what will *you* bring to the institution? Maybe it's only
your curiosity or your ability to empathize with others, but
if these have something to do with your goals, then explain
why you chose the college you're applying to and how your
ambitions will fit with the institution's mission. An applicant to a university that's known for its program in physi-

cal therapy, for example, would certainly want to express
his willingness to volunteer for that kind of work at, say,
the university hospital.

Key 5: *Write and rewrite.*
Don't send in a first draft. Make a brief outline, write a draft,
set it aside for a day or two, and then go back to it. Essays
that are tossed off in one sitting—even if they seem OK—are
often superficial. As a way of doing your own "quality control" check, read the finished essay aloud, either to yourself or to someone else. Your own ear usually will tip you
off to thoughts that are unclear or poorly expressed.

Key 6: *Type the final draft and have someone else proofread it.*
Even if your essay expresses exactly what you want the
admissions reviewer to know about you, a text that's hand-
written or marred by misspellings will undo a lot of hard
work. Keep in mind that colleges and universities maintain
standards in everything related to thinking, so don't permit
a sloppy essay to make an unfavorable statement about your
own intelligence.

Now let's read the rest of that essay written by the young man on
the commuter train, as an example of using the six keys.

If you saw me sitting near you on the commuter train
that runs through my neighborhood, you'd probably think,
Now there's a real city kid—a little tough looking, ignor-
ing everyone else, and carrying a radio. But if you looked
closer, you'd see that I was reading. And what I like to
read is just about anything that has to do with history:
19th-century novels, biographies of famous people, you
name it.

I guess I like to read about anything historical because the
past seems full of messages about what to expect in life.
Open any book about someone from long ago or even
someone still living, and you begin to understand that
your own life is some kind of story, too. Sometimes by
comparing what I'm doing to the experiences of someone in history, my own life seems to have more meaning.
Take what happened a few weeks ago, for instance.

I had just finished *The Kennedys: An American Drama,*
by Peter Collier and David Horowitz. The descriptions
of politics were so fascinating that I decided to run for
student government at school. On the day I was supposed to make my speech to the entire class, I was so
nervous I actually thought about backing out. But then I
remembered what a terrible public speaker Jack Kennedy
started out as, and that thought gave me more courage
than everyone saying, "Oh, you can do it. It'll go great."
(Incidentally, I did get elected.)

What I learned from that experience is that people grow
through facing challenges. The reason I'm applying to
your institution is that all the information you've sent me
emphasizes self-discovery. That's exactly what I want
from a college education: opportunities for challenges so
I can grow.

I'm not sure whether I'll be a historian, a teacher, or something else, but I will bring with me a desire to learn new
things about human experience. As I said earlier, I like
to read history because I want to learn what to expect in
life, and I know that your institution can help me with
that goal.

And here's one written by high school student Don Lee, in
response to Stanford University's essay question, "Suppose you
had the opportunity to spend a day with *anyone.* With whom
would it be, and how would you spend your time?"

I would love nothing more than to spend a day with
Snoopy, who, as you probably know, is the beagle in the
comic strip "Peanuts," which, as you probably do not
know, is my favorite comic strip. Snoopy is everything
and anything he wants to be—a world-famous hockey
player, a World War I flying ace, a world-famous author,
the world's best lawn sprinkler runner-througher, a world-
class figure skater, a world-famous grocery clerk. I do like
to think of my own life as rather exciting and interesting.
Nevertheless, I would like, for at least one day, to experience true thrills, to do utterly spectacular things, to be
someone utterly spectacular. Spending a day with Snoopy
would satisfy this desire. Together we would take on the

world and conquer it, climb every mountain, win every
match, charm every cute beagle, and, of course, be back
home by suppertime.

An excellent step-by-step guide on writing essays, one that your
son or daughter will find helpful is *Writing Your College
Application Essay* by Sarah Myers McGinty. The author shows
how to build a successful essay, and points out where weak
essays go astray.

Incidentally, your child should make copies of her essays and
save them. Some colleges ask the same general questions, and
reusing an essay is an accepted practice.

Obtaining Recommendations

Another step in the application process that creates uncertainty
in some students concerns recommendations. By far, recommendations are required more often by private colleges than public
ones, and they read them closely. What distinguishes a good
recommendation from a mediocre one, and whom should your
son or daughter seek out for a recommendation?

The least helpful kind of recommendation starts out by apolo-
gizing for not knowing the student well, or is written in a guarded
tone: "David has come a long way down the road to maturity
since arriving here." (But what—he still wears his clothes inside
out?) A recommendation can also be weakened if the written
portion is at variance with any boxes the writer is asked to check
as part of estimating your child's overall academic ability or his
level of maturity. It's not helpful, for instance, if the writer of a
recommendation praises your child's leadership abilities and then
rates him less than average in maturity. Finally, unhelpful recommendations depend on platitudes instead of analysis, as in: "This
young woman is really a great kid and comes from a swell family.
You're going to get a sweetheart with her." (Remember when you
were dating and somebody was recommended to you as having a
"great personality"? Same principle.)

The kind of recommendation that will shine favorably on your
child has definite characteristics: it's factual, honest and consistent;
it describes your child in the context of the classroom, the school,
or the community, and how he affects these; and it addresses
head-on any weaknesses your child may have. In addition, a good
recommendation uses descriptive words such as *motivated, ambi-
tious, curious,* and *inquisitive.*

As you can probably imagine, the most effective recommendations for your child will probably come from teachers, counselors, headmasters, principals, and coaches—but not from a congressman, for example, who may know you well but be acquainted only slightly with your son or daughter. Real understanding of a candidate distinguishes persuasive recommendations from ones that rely on faint praise.

To obtain a recommendation, here's the best method your teenager can use. First, she should request a recommendation far in advance of its due date. Being asked for a recommendation at the last minute won't put the writer in a generous frame of mind. Second, your child should give the person a deadline, so that the recommendation will be finished on time. Third, she should suggest that the writer describe her primarily in one area of school activity: as a member of the advanced placement biology class, the tennis team, or the cast of the school play. Recommendations that range too far and wide tend to become overly general. Moreover, this suggestion gives the writer a theme or focus.

To make the writer's task as easy as possible, your child should provide the person with three things: a descriptive essay about himself (similar to the first personal essay quoted, for example) that the writer can use for inspiration; a copy of the college's recommendation form (if one is provided with the application) with your child's name typed at the top; and a stamped envelope addressed to the college's admissions office.

I also suggest that your child state on the recommendation form that she waives the right to read the finished recommendation. This is a good idea because of the impact the Buckley Amendment has on recommendation writers.

The Family Rights and Privacy Act of 1974, better known among counselors and admissions specialists as the Buckley Amendment, gives enrolled or former students access to their application records, as well as other educational records, on request. The consensus on its impact can be summed up in the words of David Riesman, Harvard sociologist:

> Guidance counselors are now tremendously handicapped, in my judgment, by the Buckley Amendment, which was intended to control bias in letters of recommendation; both they and college professors suffer from the general decline in the confidentiality of records ... The result is that, in self-protection, guidance officials write blandly praising letters, which are discarded as worthless.

If your child is confident that he will receive a strong recommendation from someone, waiving the right to see it probably will result in a more thorough appraisal, and the admissions office will know it was written with complete candor.

After your child has given the blank recommendation form to someone, he should make tactful checks on that person's progress. When the deadline is approaching, he should call the admissions office to check whether or not the form has been received. Afterwards, a thank-you note to the writer is in order, and it's also considerate to let the writer know the outcome of the application. If your child balks at going to these lengths, remind him that he may have to call on that person again, perhaps even several times.

As busy as your child may be in assembling all the components of the application, she must not forget to request an official transcript from her high school registrar's office and have it sent to the college. Some high schools will pair the transcript with your child's application and mail them in one envelope. Others leave it to the applicant to mail the application on her own. In any case, your child cannot mail the transcript herself—if she does, it won't be considered an official record of coursework by an admissions office.

One more piece of advice: as long as we're being careful to do things right, I recommend that your child make a photocopy of the application for his file and then send the original by certified mail. That way a receipt will be returned when the application arrives, and your child will have a record that he met the deadline.

Handling The Personal Interview

Well, is that everything? Hopefully, but what if the college's admissions office either requires or "strongly encourages" a personal interview at some point during the application process?

If your child is offered the opportunity to interview, she should take it. Moreover, why should she wait to be contacted? No admissions interviewer will take it amiss if your child calls first to arrange an interview. Just the opposite—such ambition will be to her credit. A good interview can offset weaknesses in other areas of her credentials, and it's the rare candidate who doesn't have at least a couple of weaknesses. Statistically, interviewing does pay off. Grinnell College (IA), using figures from East Coast applicants for the 1982-83 school year, reported "the percentage denied of noninterviewed applicants was twice that for applicants interviewed."

Usually, interviews can be arranged in one of two ways. Either the applicant makes an appointment for an interview at the admissions office or—if the candidate can't come to campus—an alumnus will interview him at a convenient place. When the interview is held on campus, parents are always welcome, although you probably will be asked to wait in another room until invited in. Interviewers are interested in the relationship between you and your child, so ask questions, but let your son or daughter take the lead. Try not to take the role of your child's "translator."

A good personal interview will cover your teenager's long-range goals and special interests. Areas commonly touched on will be academic skills and educational background, motivational characteristics such as preferences and ambitions, and personality strengths and weaknesses. Some routine questions include:

▶ How are you enjoying high school?

▶ What are your favorite classes and why?

▶ Describe one of the best teachers you've had.

▶ What's one of the best books you've read?

▶ What do you like to do outside of class?

▶ Why are you considering this institution?

▶ What other schools are you applying to?

▶ Do you have any questions you'd like to ask?

Keep in mind it's not the intention of a good interviewer to make your child feel uncomfortable. As a very skillful interviewer once told me, "I think it's my job to help applicants remember the best things about themselves. I'm not here to sit in judgment, or to make someone feel inadequate. What I hope will come out during the interview are indications that this person will thrive here and that we'll be glad if she decides to enroll."

Occasionally, however, applicants make things tough on themselves during the interview process for the following reasons:

Lateness: Not allowing time to find a parking space—or the admissions office—can result in your child arriving flustered and apologetic. Having to spend 15 minutes flipping through magazines in the outer office is better than arriving 15 minutes late.

Undefined educational goals: Some students go into interviews without having given serious thought to their goals. While most interviewers may be willing to provide advice, it's not appropriate for them to help applicants resolve important questions about their plans. A student's educational goals and objectives should be worked out ahead of time with the help of family members or a high school guidance counselor.

Lack of knowledge about the institution: By the time candidates are at the interview stage, they should not have to ask whether the college has a business program, or request other types of information that they should have gleaned from reading the catalog. I remember sitting in on an interview once during which the candidate said she was interested in a preveterinary program. Unfortunately, the college didn't offer one, and the interview ground to a rather sudden halt.

If you'd like to help your child prepare for an interview, role playing can be effective. Casting yourself in the role of the admissions interviewer, use the list of questions provided earlier or make up your own. Listen carefully to your child's responses. Make suggestions, but be supportive and not overly critical. Not only will this kind of practice help your child to think through his responses, but the rehearsal will probably boost his confidence at the actual interview.

And now, what exactly will an admissions office do with all the information it has drawn from your child? How are decisions made to accept some applicants and deny others?

CHAPTER 10

Let's Sit In on an Admissions Committee

None may expect to be admitted into the College but
such as being examined by the Presidents and Tutors,
shall be found able to render Virgil and Tully's orations
into English and to turn English into true and grammatical Latin: and be so well acquainted with the Greek as
to render any part of the four Evangelists in that language into Latin or English and to give the grammatical
construction of the words.

So read the regulations for admission to Princeton University 150 years ago. At one time so few people could aspire
to higher education that in 1841, the student body at the
University of Michigan stood at seven. But by the early 1960s,
a large institution could reasonably expect 19,000 applications
for 5,200 places in the freshman class.

Today, colleges are meeting the demand for higher education by staffing their admissions offices with people who have
expertise in human relations, direct mail marketing, and staff
development. Directors of admissions use computer software
programs to predict enrollment, and representatives offer glimpses
of their campuses by means of videotape, slide show, or laser
disc. Nevertheless they, like their predecessors, continue to
have one main responsibility: to apply standards that are intended to admit only applicants who can complete their education
successfully.

The variety of admission standards being practiced (as described in Chapter 4) might make you wonder who sets the
requirements. In most instances, it's the institution's chief execu-

tive officer or a specially appointed admissions committee who sets them. Interestingly, more than one-third of four-year colleges include students on their admissions policy committees. Ultimately, however, the director of admissions has some flexibility within prescribed guidelines, and in many cases can override decisions of the committee.

The Selection Process

The selection process itself is really not very complicated. The majority of institutions choose the most qualified applicants on a first-come, first-served basis until enough applicants have been accepted to fill the class.

At both public and private institutions, an admissions reader reviewing an application asks himself two questions: Does the candidate meet the standards of the institution? And, does he meet the standards of the program he wishes to enter? By weighing the answers, the reader must come to a decision based, to some degree, on an estimation of the applicant's probable academic success.

How Credentials Are Weighed

Let's look more closely now at how specific credentials are usually weighed at institutions with liberal, traditional, and selective admissions policies (see Chapter 4).

In most instances, the information your child submits about herself will be ranked, in order of importance, as follows: grade-point average, rank in class, test scores, and quality of coursework. Although test scores matter slightly more to public institutions than to private schools, both types generally agree that scores should be used to confirm or contradict impressions made by the applicant's other credentials; by themselves, test scores don't mean a great deal. Concerning coursework, colleges invariably prefer applicants who have challenged themselves to the greatest extent.

As you might expect, recommendations, interviews, and personal essays carry much more weight with private institutions, most of which want to admit students who will be compatible with the school's unique character. As we saw in Chapter 9, an evaluation of the personal essay will favor examples of proven ability, academic or otherwise, which include having overcome obstacles such as social prejudice, inadequate schooling, a poor home environment, physical handicaps, personal challenges, or otherwise adverse circumstances.

Participation in extracurricular activities and the earning of awards and distinctions come lower on the list of priorities for both private and public colleges. In these areas, the reviewer will look for contributions to the community, a talent for leadership, adeptness in competitive sports, or special ability in music, acting, writing, or some other endeavor.

Sometimes, factors that would not technically qualify as credentials may also be taken under consideration. For example, can the candidate contribute to the institution's racial, ethnic, or geographic diversity? By being admitted, will the candidate help maintain an "attractive" male/female ratio? Also, since many institutions have a legal obligation to admit a high percentage of taxpayers' children, is the applicant an in-state resident? The son or daughter of an alumnus has a slight advantage too, especially at private institutions—these candidates are sometimes referred to as "legacies."

Mechanics of the Selection Process

Now that you have a general understanding of the credentials weighed by most institutions, a look at the mechanics of the selection process may be of interest.

Review committees almost always start with a close review of all the applicant's credentials: his test scores, recommendations, and the quality of his coursework, for instance. Applicants' folders are read and reread as they circulate through the admissions office in a regular pattern. Readers at some schools use a letter system—say, A through E—to divide applications into groups. Others use numbers.

Many readers add written comments, not only to more easily bring about a consensus but also to serve as a future reference in case a denied applicant asks for an explanation. Next, folders are usually placed into three broad categories: superior, average, and doubtful. Then the folders in each category are often reevaluated to pinpoint candidates whose files warrant closer scrutiny: scholarship candidates, applicants with unexpectedly low test scores, and others with special circumstances. The latter might include students who have changed schools many times, or who recently arrived in the United States. In clear-cut cases, the director will sign off *yes* or *no*. Difficult cases will often go to a committee, which is usually composed of faculty members and administrators and occasionally includes students and alumni (more about this later in the chapter).

After all cases have been reviewed and the number of accepted applicants is enough to fill the freshman class, action letters (letters of acceptance) are sent, and the wait begins. This is a nervous time for admissions directors, because even the most competent ones must rely partly on instinct when it comes to estimating how many accepted candidates will actually arrive on campus.

Review by Highly Selective Schools

The scenario is not much different even at highly selective institutions (which constitute about 1 in 10 of all colleges and universities). The same sort of care is taken to read and reread credentials. The only major difference is that these readers weigh heavily a number of nonacademic factors, that is, recommendations, extracurricular activities, and personal characteristics. They search for subtler indications of outstanding motivation, creativity, or accomplishment. The emphasis here is placed equally on academic and personal potential.

What's frustrating to some applicants and their parents is that these standards seem so mysterious. And they're right in a sense, for as selectivity increases, specific explanations for rejection are less obvious. During late winter and early spring, for example, the Harvard-Radcliffe admissions staff meets to select 2,000 out of 13,000 applicants. There are two "cuts." The first is based totally on academics, and *most* of the candidates make it. The second evaluation examines personal qualities and strengths. From here on in, selection is something of an art. As the committee wrote in its 1984-85 bulletin to high school counselors, " . . . the Admissions Committee looks for independent thinking, intellectual curiosity and thoughtful questioning, tenacity and resilience, the motivation to pursue a liberal arts education, and the ability to use the resources of the University well." From this description it's difficult to extract any kind of "formula" for acceptance to a highly selective school.

If your child is applying to institutions with liberal, traditional, or selective admissions policies, however, you may find useful the following list of often-asked questions about admissions practices.

Questions about Admissions Practices

▶ *Do colleges just look for high grades?*

The big selling point about good grades is that they indicate a willingness to work in various types of courses. But a poor grade or two will not ruin your son's or daughter's chances. After all, few people are equally strong in all subjects. Also, grades that show improvement, even at a late date, are looked on favorably.

▶ *My daughter doesn't usually test well—how will an admissions person know that?*

Admissions officials appreciate the vagaries of testing: the mood of the student at the time, the possibility that the student is a slow reader, and so forth. That is why other criteria—grades, class rank, recommendations, and nonacademic indications of potential—are taken into account. As I mentioned earlier, test scores are evaluated in conjunction with other pieces of information. When admissions personnel come across test scores that are significantly out of step, especially ones that are lower than what an applicant's grades would predict, they are careful to weigh them in light of the total profile presented by the applicant's other credentials.

▶ *Do colleges give preference to children from families that have donated to the school?*

College administrators know that heat and light and lab equipment are not free; consequently, they are grateful for gifts. Candidly speaking, there must be times when accepting the offer of a donation is viewed in terms of what would benefit an institution in the long run. But no donation will be accepted on condition that a particular student be admitted, no questions asked.

▶ *What about children of alumni—are they given special treatment?*

For financial reasons, private colleges and universities often have special admissions programs for children of alumni or faculty. These applicants are sometimes offered reduced tuition rates, or occasionally will still be considered for admission after the official deadline has passed. As I said in Chapter 5, private institutions must do what they can to encourage loyalty among alumni and supporters because their competition—public colleges and universities—usually enjoy more political support in the form of tuition subsidies. Public institutions aren't usually in the position of having to give children of alumni special consideration.

▶ *Are admissions standards lower for minority students?*

In a recent survey of a representative sampling of colleges and universities, 37 percent said they might apply less rigorous standards to applications from racial or ethnic minority students, or disadvantaged students. Note, however, this means that the majority do not lower their standards. (For more information about minority students, see Chapter 8.)

▶ *Do my child's extracurricular activities in high school count for anything?*

Yes, as long as grades have not suffered as a result. As we discussed in Chapter 9, students with a variety of interests are attractive to most colleges, especially liberal arts institutions. But colleges prefer applicants who have participated in depth in a few activities. It's a myth that colleges esteem only the well-rounded student who's a "jack-of-all-trades" and, as the saying goes, "master of none."

▶ Scenes From Admissions Committee Meetings

Let's conclude with a look at those "difficult cases" we touched on earlier. I take you now to a meeting of an admissions committee at a selective university, one that requires above-average grades and test scores, supported by strong recommendations. What follows is an actual discussion that took place when the committee met to review promising candidates whose applications, for one reason or another, had serious problems. Only a few details about the applicants have been changed for the sake of confidentiality.

Case 1: The Lazy Essayist

The committee, made up of six admissions people and two faculty members, is gathered around a large mahogany table in the office of the director of admissions. This kind of discussion is never easy; the applicants under consideration are all competitive but have fallen into the "marginal" category, usually through some lack of effort on their part. The first case is a good example. Assistant Director of Admissions Mark Anderson explains the situation.

"This student is eighth out of sixty in a private school in upstate New York. His ACT is above average. Most of his grades are A's. His counselor recommendation mentions 'high ability,' 'tackles problems,' and 'leadership.' He's also a soccer player and our coaches are interested in him."

Director of Admissions Hal Dannenfeld asks, "So what's the problem?"

"He completely blew the personal essay," says Anderson. "It's brief, lazy-sounding—obviously no thought was put into it. I called the boy's counselor, who said he saw the essay and told the boy to 'do better,' but it came in like this anyway."

Dannenfeld acts disgusted. "So we're supposed to take this application seriously? How can we? We've sent representatives to that school for years. They know our standards."

Associate Director Neil Edwards speaks up. "So instead we punish him by denying him admission? Normally we would admit him on the face of his credentials. My question is, if he did the work, can we make the assumption that he won't work hard here? We seem to be drawing a very negative conclusion based on one half-hearted essay."

"Neil, he exercised a choice," says Dannenfeld. "He chose not to try. He apparently didn't care enough to put some work into the application."

Jacqueline Zinsser, also an associate director, suggests a compromise. "Let's ask for a graded paper from his senior English class to replace the essay. But I have to say that I have a big problem with someone who gets A's in English and sends us an essay that's been dashed off."

The committee votes to request a graded paper that will replace the essay.

Case 2: The Weak Recommendation

The next application was from a girl about to graduate from a medium-size rural school in Michigan.

"This girl's transcript is strong," says Zinsser. "She's taken a number of honors classes and her grades were mainly A's and B's. Her counselor calls her 'outstanding,' but the box checked under Intellectual Ability is *Good,* not *Excellent.* Also, she's never been involved in any extracurricular activities." "What about recommendations?" says Dannenfeld.

"Well, that's part of the problem. You'd think she'd go out and get the strongest ones she could, to offset any weaknesses in the application. But she got just one recommendation, from her minister, and it was only lukewarm. She didn't waive the right to see it, so I suspect she read it and sent it anyway."

Dannenfeld rubs his forehead. "Sounds like an application where some kind of problem only surfaces in bits and pieces. Her counselor chooses *Good* instead of *Excellent*. She's not involved in anything at school and the only recommendation that's submitted seems to back away a little bit. She could have reassured us by getting a few rec's that were solid and enthusiastic. I say no."

The vote goes one for acceptance, seven for denial.

Case 3: The Inconsistent Student

The last application has been submitted by a very bright student. Edwards outlines the problem:

"This boy's father is a physician. The boy ranks ninetieth out of 356. His SAT scores are 500 verbal and a 740 math, which is pretty exceptional. He's getting an A in Advanced English, but wait. His essay is full of horrible misspellings such as 'collage' for 'college' and 'conferance' for 'conference.' Also, our alumnus who interviewed him said this student really couldn't defend his choice of nuclear physics as an area of study. And last, his science grades aren't outstanding, but he told the interviewer he thought the 740 math score would compensate for that."

"His science grades aren't outstanding?" says Dannenfeld. "With a 740 math? They should be exceptional!"

"I think it's pretty clear what's going on," says Zinsser. "On a day-to-day basis this applicant coasts along in class, and then when it's time to take the SAT he really tries and pulls out a 740. But that's a strong indication that he wouldn't try very hard here unless he had to. I vote no."

The committee votes unanimously against acceptance. Perhaps there's a moral here: scores aren't everything.

I hope that by sitting in on these actual admissions decisions, you understand better how your child's application will be evaluated. Now, however, it's time to leave the admissions office and move to one where the decisions made will also influence which institution your child attends—the financial aid office.

CHAPTER 11

Everything You Need to Know about Financial Aid

Since 1643, when an English noblewoman created a fund at Harvard for needy students, financial aid for college in the United States has increased to well over $16 billion a year, or enough to send a quarter of a million students through Harvard. Approximately half of all college students and three-quarters of low-income students receive financial aid of some type through state, federal, or private sources.

Over the last decade, however, a problem has been developing: student aid has not been keeping up with rising college costs. In fact, in recent years, the real value of student aid has declined by 21 percent. But before you assume that financial aid is shrinking out of sight, or that it's not worth going after in any case, let's tackle a few misconceptions that tend to discourage people from seeking financial aid.

One of the most common is that financial aid is intended only for poor people. Actually, its purpose is to remove financial barriers for families who cannot afford the cost of an education beyond high school, and for those who can afford to pay only part of it. The reasons a family might be in either of these circumstances can be tied to many particulars—the parents' age, the amount of their home mortgage, whether they have other children in college—each of which is taken into consideration by financial aid administrators. Financial aid, then, is not out of reach strictly because you "make too much."

Secondly, many parents believe they can afford only low-priced colleges because their resources are limited. But the truth is that the more expensive institutions, which are generally private, offer competitive amounts of financial aid to attract students from all income levels. In fact, if you suspect that you qualify for aid, the more expensive college might be a better bargain: the greater the gap between your resources and the cost of an institution, the greater the likelihood of aid (part of which may be in the form of "gift aid," or grants as they're called).

"I still don't think it's fair," a parent said to me recently. "I saved a long time for my son's college education, and then the guy across the street, who never put away a dime, told me his daughter is going to get all the financial aid she needs to attend a private university. How can that be right?"

Fair or not, financial aid is very often available to those *who make the effort* to apply. Money is not awarded automatically—it must be applied for by families. Not even renewal of an award is automatic. A family must apply each year. Sound difficult? It's not, if you keep in mind that lining up financial aid requires three things:

▶ A commitment to make a thorough search

▶ An understanding of how financial aid works

▶ Attention to detail and follow-up

While the purpose of this chapter is to tell you how to apply for aid, keep in mind that "financial aid is not an entitlement program," as Natala Hart, former vice president for Student Assistance Services of the College Board, observes. "The first obligation to pay for college still lies with the family."

Overview of Financial Aid

Let's start with some basic terms and definitions. *Financial aid* is offered as a means of helping college students meet educational expenses. Funds for financial aid come from the state and federal governments, commercial banks, the college itself, and outside sources you may contact on your own.

When a student receives aid, it usually comes in one or more of three forms: *scholarships* or *grants,* which are outright gifts of money that do not have to be repaid; *loans,* which can be repaid after graduation; and *work-study,* a job arranged for a student during the academic year to cover part of his expenses. *Expenses* include tuition, room and board, books and supplies, transportation costs (visits home included), and miscellaneous fees such as application fee, activity fee, room key deposit, room damage deposit, auto registration fee, and locker fee.

Most financial aid is made available on the basis of *financial need*. Financial need is the difference between the estimated expenses of college and what a family can contribute. To take a simple example: if your family can contribute $3,000 toward a year of college that costs a total of $8,000, then your financial need is $5,000. Naturally, determining whether or not your child demonstrates need requires more information about your family than just a ballpark estimate on how much you think you can afford. Instead, you must provide a financial profile of your household, including such factors as income, assets, debts, retirement needs, family size, and number of students in college. From this information an evaluation will be made, using a set of formulas called the Congressional Methodology, adopted as part of the Higher Education Amendments of 1986. Although the formulas used for calculating a family's contribution are revised annually, the Congressional Methodology continues to be based on five general principles:

1) Parents have an obligation to finance the education of their children to the extent that they are able.

2) A family's income and assets combined produce a comprehensive index of the family's financial strength and its capacity to contribute to educational costs.

3) Factors such as family size, extraordinary expenses, age of the parents, and other considerations must be weighed in relation to income and asset information in order to measure a family's true ability to pay for an education.

4) Students and their families must be accepted in their present financial condition; that is, the objective facts of a family's financial situation must be examined to determine the family's ability to pay.

5) Students have a responsibility to help pay for their own education and, as primary beneficiaries of that education, should contribute a proportionately greater share of their income and assets than should their parents.

In some instances, special circumstances will make a difference as to whether or not your teenager receives aid. For example, aid for your child would depend on the amount of funds actually available from various sources: College A might be in a position to allocate a substantial amount of aid money every year to helping applicants, whereas College B cannot. The needs of other applicants may also affect you: colleges often make awards in order of need—and when the money runs out, it's gone, whether or not everyone has received assistance. Furthermore, the specific program to which your child is applying sometimes makes a difference. Programs in the health professions, for example, may have special federal funds designated for student assistance.

If your child can demonstrate need, he will probably receive help in the form of a *financial aid package,* which can include any combination of grants, loans, and work. By law, most federal aid must be awarded on the basis of need. However, a thorough search can often uncover sources of college funding that are available without regard to need. For example, an increasing number of colleges, in order to maintain their enrollment of middle-income students, have begun offering *merit awards.* These are given solely on the basis of talent or scholarship, without regard to need. Likewise, some colleges will award larger grants and smaller loans in the financial aid package to a student who received more A's than B's in high school, once again rewarding ability without regard to need.

Now that I've given you an overview of financial aid, let's walk, step by step, through the application process.

Assembling Information

The first step in beginning your campaign is to assemble information that will help answer your questions ahead of time and make the application process easier. Here are several free publications about financial aid, each updated annually:

> *Applying for Financial Aid,* ACT Publications, P.O. Box 168, Iowa City, IA 52243.
> *Meeting College Costs,* The College Scholarship Service, available through high school guidance offices.
> *The Student Guide: Five Federal Financial Aid Programs,* Consumer Information Center, Pueblo, CO 81009.

Other publications you may wish to consult are:

> *The College Cost Book,* College Board Publications, P.O. Box 886, New York, NY 10101.

Financial Aids for Higher Education, 1988-89, Oreon Kees-
lar, editor, 13th ed. Dubuque, IA: Wm. C. Brown Company, 1988. Updated biennially. More than 3,000 programs are listed specifically for students entering as
college freshmen.

Foundation Grants to Individuals, Loren Renz, editor, 5th
ed. New York: Foundation Center, 1986. Undergraduate
and graduate scholarship sources are categorized under
general and specific requirements. Also included are fellowships, residences, internships, and grants by United
States foundations to foreign nationals or citizens, as well
as company-sponsored aid programs.

Getting Yours: The Complete Guide to Government Money by
Matthew Lesko. New York: Penguin Books, 1987. Many
of the federal government programs listed in the Office of
Management and Budget's Catalog of Federal Domestic
Assistance are summarized here, including grants, schol-
arships, and fellowships.

Need a Lift? Indianapolis: The American Legion, 1988. Updated annually. Sources of career, scholarship, and loan
information for all students are listed, with emphasis on
scholarship opportunities for veterans, their dependents,
and children of deceased or disabled veterans.

Student Aid Annual, 1988-89. Moravia, NY: Chronicle Guidance Publications, Inc., 1988. Financial aid programs for
students at undergraduate and graduate levels of study
are listed, including those offered by noncollege organizations, labor unions, and federal and state governments.

Next, take a look at how your family handles its finances in
light of what you might be expected to pay toward college
costs. For information about how the Tax Reform Act of 1986
affects savings, investment, and income-shifting strategies, as
well as how to structure a personal financial planning program
for covering college costs, the following book provides useful
guidelines:

How to Pay for Your Children's College Education by Gerald
Krefetz, College Board Publications, P.O. Box 886, New
York, NY 10101.

You needn't go it alone either when it comes to reviewing your
family's finances. A route to consider is having an accountant
prepare your return. Accountants are trained and, in some states,
licensed professionals whose services are usually listed in the
Yellow Pages.

Once you've gotten your feet wet by reading up on the application process, it's a good idea to estimate beforehand the amount of aid necessary to finance your child's education. For a rough estimate, subtract your probable family financial contribution from the total costs of the colleges you're considering. Costs include all of the things listed earlier in the chapter—tuition, books, and so on—plus an allowance of $1,000 a year for personal expenses.

Rearranging your personal finances

As the College Board points out in *The College Cost Book*, "Few families can cover their expected share of college costs from current earnings only, never mind bridge the gap that could be created by insufficient financial aid resources. To minimize the impact on your household budget when the time comes to start paying college bills, you should start planning as early as possible.

"For instance, you might want to think about how your current assets can be resources for paying educational bills. Ask yourself, What are they worth now? What are they most likely to be worth when I want to use them? You may want to talk to your banker, a financial adviser, or an investment specialist about the best way of 'saving' for college, given your financial situation. These professionals can offer you advice on financial planning for college based on your present situation, how much time you have left to save, and the risks involved in selecting certain financing alternatives.

"The Tax Reform Act of 1986 changed some of the rules governing ways in which families can accumulate money for college. There are several guides to the new tax law available in bookstores, and you can also pose questions directly to the local office of the Internal Revenue Service (IRS). Or you may want to seek the help of a professional adviser, such as a Certified Financial Planner (CFP), a Certified Public Accountant (CPA), or a tax attorney. In any case, carefully investigate all the features of the programs offered by banks and investment firms. There is considerable variety in the safety, the yield, and the requirements of college savings programs and products now on the market. Shop around before you invest your hard-earned dollars. Even if you have to start paying bills within the next year, it is worth your time to talk to your banker about your current savings and investment arrangements.

"No college expects you to sell the family homestead to pay for education, but some colleges *are* becoming quite explicit about their expectations of families with assets. You may find that a college financial aid office wants to know your net return on investments, for instance. Others may suggest that you refinance the mortgage on your home. Others may inquire about the contribution that other members of the extended family (such as grandparents) might make to a student's educational expenses. Such observations from colleges may startle or even anger you, but they reflect a renewed emphasis on the family's central responsibility for financing education or training after high school."

Financial Aid Applications

As soon as your child reaches the fall of his senior year, he should obtain the necessary aid information from each institution he's considering. Usually this information will be automatically sent with an application, which by now your teenager should have. Many schools have their own financial aid application, which asks how much assistance you think you might require. These colleges do their own analysis so they can anticipate what kinds of demands might be made on their funds. By helping them to plan, you may be benefiting your child in the long run.

Next, your child can lend a hand by finding out which state and federal aid forms her college choices prefer. She should check each institution's own catalog or a college handbook. The forms will usually be available in her high school guidance department by mid-November, but you should not submit them until after January 1, because they will otherwise be returned. Financial aid agencies insist that you wait until the year has ended before supplying information about your household (you might receive a big holiday bonus, for example). If you have trouble locating the forms, phone the colleges' financial aid offices. Remember—you need to file separate forms for each child in college, even if they are attending the same school.

The two most widely required financial aid forms are the Family Financial Statement (FFS) and the Financial Aid Form (FAF). These are actually services offered to colleges, the first by the American College Test (ACT), and the second by the College Scholarship Service of the College Board (some institutions subscribe to both services). The data provided by applicants is

interpreted for campus aid administrators, making it easi
them to compare the financial backgrounds of various candi
In addition, as was mentioned earlier, colleges require the data
collected by the FFS or FAF before they can even consider
candidates for institutionally controlled funds.

If you don't use the FFS and FAF, some schools may require
that you complete the U.S. Department of Education's Application for Federal Student Aid (AFSA); in Pennsylvania you're
required to complete the Pennsylvania Higher Education Assistance Agency's (PHEAA) Application for Pennsylvania State
Grant and Federal Student Aid; and in California completion
of the Student Aid Application for California (SAAC) is required.
Each of these, like the FFS and FAF, contains a question or
statement asking whether you wish to be considered for federal
financial aid. Check "Yes." The question or statement is near the
end of the application in the "Other Information" or "Release"
section.

Questions Often Asked

Before you start completing any of the forms, read the instructions.
There are pointers on how to approach certain sections, and
phone numbers you can call for assistance. Here are some questions parents often ask:

▶ *Must my child be accepted at a college before we can apply
for aid?*

No. Submit the institution's application for financial aid
at the same time your child applies for admission. Submit
the FFS, FAF, or any of the others as soon after January 1
as possible.

▶ *My eldest child was turned down for aid last year. Should
I go through the whole process again for the child who's
entering college this year?*

Yes. In fact, the likelihood of your family receiving aid will
increase because you will have two children in college. Also,
college costs, institutional policies, and your own financial
circumstances change from year to year.

▶ *Are noncitizens eligible for aid?*

Noncitizens who are permanent residents are eligible for
state or federal aid; in most cases, noncitizens who are not
permanent residents are not eligible. Some colleges, however, do have institutional funds available for noncitizens
who are not permanent residents.

▶ *My daughter is applying for a scholarship only. Does she
have to file any of the forms mentioned earlier?*

She should check with the scholarship sponsor and the financial aid office of the college where the scholarship will be
used.

▶ *My husband and I are divorced. Who should fill out
the form?*

The parent with whom the child has lived the longest during the preceding 12 months should file. If the time spent
with either parent has been about equal, then the parent
who has supplied the most support—food, clothing,
housing, medical and dental care—should be the one to
file. Some colleges may require both parents to file
forms and/or provide financial information.

▶ *My husband is my son's stepparent, but he says he doesn't
feel obligated to pay for his college education. Will he be
expected to file a form?*

If you are the parent required to complete the forms,
your husband must also provide financial information.

▶ *My wife and I are separated, and my daughter lives
with her. Yet she refuses to supply the information my
daughter needs to apply for aid. I'm willing to do this, so
can I file instead?*

For your daughter to apply for federal aid, your wife must
supply the necessary data. But if this isn't possible, the aid
administrator at the college to which your child is ap-

plying may decide that since adverse circumstances prevent the required information from being obtained, information from you will be acceptable. These circumstances should be described on the form, or in a letter to the college. Do not, however, attempt to correspond with the college via the need analysis agency. Write to the college's financial aid office directly. You will probably be unable to receive federal or state aid without the required documentation, but the college may be able to help you with some of its own private funds.

▶ *I'm a foster parent and the child staying with me is a ward of the state. Do I file for aid?*

A ward of the state is considered an independent student and should file his or her own application for aid (you can help with the paperwork, of course).

▶ *Do my wife and I have to wait until we file our income tax return before we apply for financial aid?*

No, but wait until you've received your W-2 forms and other relevant financial statements. If information changes after you have completed your tax return, you will have an opportunity to revise the information you provided on the original form. Read the form's instructions on making revisions.

▶ *Should I attach a copy of my IRS Form 1040 to the aid application?*

No, not unless a college requests a copy to validate information you supplied. You should be aware, however, that colleges do extensive verification, and you could be asked to provide tax returns or other additional information. Deliberately supplying misinformation on an aid form carries penalties ranging from loss of aid and repayment of any funds received, to fines and/or imprisonment.

▶ *My husband and I established a trust fund for my son, but he can't touch it until he turns 21. Do we have to report it when we apply for aid?*

Yes, because it's part of your financial strength.

▶ *What is untaxed income?*

Untaxed income is any income you receive that is not subject to U.S. income taxes. This includes such things as Social Security payments and veterans benefits, welfare, child support, untaxed pensions, and military subsistence allowance. Specific questions you have concerning untaxed income should be directed to the college's financial aid office.

▶ *Will my child be considered for state scholarships or aid by filing either the FFS or the FAF?*

In many cases, yes. Check with your high school guidance department on whether or not you need a state-specific form for financial aid.

Here are some tips that will help prevent delays in the processing of your application:

▶ Get your son or daughter a Social Security number. This is necessary to be considered for federal aid.

▶ Don't wait until far into the winter to file: estimate your taxes and income as soon as possible after January 1.

▶ Indicate the actual amount in your checking and savings accounts on the day you complete the form.

▶ Estimate the worth of your residence as the amount it could be sold for on the day the form is submitted.

▶ Check for inconsistent numbers (you can't list your income as zero and have paid taxes, too).

▶ Check to be certain veterans benefits and Social Security payments are accurately reported.

▶ Although a section is provided on some forms (such as the FAF) in which to explain special circumstances, attach no documents (receipts, bank statements, and so on) until requested to do so.

▶ Make sure you list the code numbers of the schools and programs from which you child wants to receive financial aid.

▶ Sign the form and address it properly.

▶ Put the right amount of postage on the envelope.

▶ Keep a photocopy of all applications and forms.

The Acknowledgment Report

After the Financial Aid Form is received by the College Scholarship Service or the Family Financial Statement by the ACT, your family's financial information will be analyzed according to formulas. You will then be sent an acknowledgment report. At this point, you have the opportunity to correct the data you provided or add the code numbers of additional colleges. If you filed an FAF, along with the acknowledgment form you will receive a preliminary estimate of your family's expected financial contribution.

At about the same time you receive an acknowledgement report, the colleges you listed on the application for aid will also receive reports. This is an important step, because regardless of where aid money originates, most of it is channeled through campus financial aid offices. So if you have questions about the status of your application, phone the colleges' financial aid offices—you won't be hurting your child's chances of receiving aid.

Meanwhile, what's going on at the financial aid offices of the colleges that automatically received reports around the same time as you did? The financial aid administrator at each will compare your Expected Family Contribution to the cost of attending his institution, and if your family still has need, he will attempt to put together an aid package from among a number of programs and resources. The first avenues he will turn to are the federally sponsored programs.

The Pell Grant/Student Aid Report

Four to six weeks after submitting your aid application, you will receive a Student Aid Report (SAR) from the Pell Grant processing center. All applicants for federal financial aid are required to apply for assistance from the Pell Grant fund, the largest federal grant program (you apply for a Pell Grant automatically when you indicate on the aid application that you want to be considered for federal aid). Currently, the maximum your child can receive is $2,100.

The SAR contains the information you gave on your aid application. Based on that information, a Student Aid Index number is calculated, and this number will appear on your SAR. Your child's eligibility for a Pell Grant depends on this number. The lower the number is, the more likely it is that your child will be eligible. The next step is to send a photocopy of both sides of Part 1 of your SAR to the financial aid office at each school to which your child has applied. Eventually, when your teenager decides which school he is going to attend, submit all three parts of the SAR to that school's financial aid administrator. He will use the Student Aid Index to determine the amount of your son's Pell Grant. The college will credit this amount to an account established for your child at the beginning of the school year or on a term-by-term basis. The sum will be deducted from your child's tuition, fees, and other school charges.

If, say, two months have passed since you filed for aid and you have not received an SAR, phone the federal processing center at (800) 333-INFO between 9 a.m. and 5:30 p.m. (Eastern Standard Time) Monday through Friday.

Federally Sponsored Aid Programs

Supplemental Educational Opportunity Grant

The Supplemental Educational Opportunity Grant (SEOG) is a federally funded, institutionally awarded grant. This means that the college receives a sum of money from the federal government, which it then disburses to help needy students. Awards range from $100 to $4,000 per academic year and can be renewed, pending continued evidence of financial need, satisfactory academic progress, and adequate funding levels.

Perkins Loan Program

The Perkins Loan Program, formerly called the National Direct Student Loan (NDSL) is a campus-based federal loan program through which your child is able to borrow up to $9,000 for undergraduate study. Repayment of the loan is made to the college and begins six months after your child is no longer enrolled at least half-time, at an annual interest rate of 5 percent. Your son or daughter is eligible to defer payment of both principal and interest while enrolled in graduate school or serving in the military or the Peace Corps. Partial cancellation may be awarded for teaching in certain federally designated, low-income areas. Repayment may take up to 10 years depending on the amount of the principal.

College Work-Study

College Work-Study help is awarded to students who demonstrate significant financial need. This federal program allows qualified students to earn part of their college expenses. If your child is eligible, she will be sent for employment interviews at the beginning of the academic year, and probably will be permitted to work as many as 40 hours a week, although 10 to 15 hours a week is more typical. Work opportunities, which pay the minimum hourly wage, vary from employment in the campus food service facility to responsibility as a laboratory assistant.

Guaranteed Student Loan

Under the Guaranteed Student Loan (GSL) program (renamed Stafford Student Loans in 1988), community lending institutions (banks, savings and loans, credit unions) make funding available for college expenses. The maximum amount freshmen and sophomores may borrow is $2,625 per academic year. Upperclassmen may borrow up to $4,000 annually. Repayment begins six months after your son or daughter is no longer enrolled at least half-time, at an annual interest rate of 8 percent. He or she is eligible to defer payment of both principal and interest while enrolled in graduate school or serving in the military or the Peace Corps.

All GSL applicants must demonstrate financial need, and the amount of need may limit the amount of your GSL. Ask the colleges your child is considering how to initiate the GSL application process.

Start looking for lenders early and complete your part of the application at least six to eight weeks before the start of school. Your child will have to sign a promissory note for the loan and arrange to receive the check. The federal government allows lenders to withhold 5 percent of the loan amount as an "origination fee" and you may also be charged by your state guarantee agency for an insurance premium.

Parents Loans for Undergraduate Students

The Parents Loans for Undergraduate Students (PLUS) program allows you, as the parent of a dependent student, to borrow up to $4,000 annually to finance educational expenses for each dependent child. Eligibility is based on your child's enrollment at a minimum half-time status and on the difference between the annual cost of attendance and the amount of any financial aid you might have received. You do not have to demonstrate need, but you may have to undergo a credit analysis. Repayment begins 60 days after you've received the funds and is due at an annual interest rate based on the treasury bill rate plus 3.25 percentage points up to a maximum of 12 percent. The loan amount is paid by check directly to you. PLUS is often used as a solution to cash flow problems.

Although PLUS is available in most states, if you have difficulty locating a participating lender, contact a local college financial aid office.

Institutional Aid Programs

After determining whether your child is eligible for any of the federally sponsored programs, a financial aid administrator will then consider your son or daughter for institutional awards. As was noted earlier, many colleges and universities recently introduced "no-need merit awards" based on talent or scholarship. A hypothetical example would be one we'll call the Mountain College Presidential Scholarship. Its criteria might be that an applying student be in the upper quarter of her high school graduating class and have received at least 25 on the ACT, or 1080 on the SAT. All entering students who met these criteria would receive the scholarship.

Next, the aid administrator will see whether your child is eligible for any other institutional awards, such as (let's make up another one) the Edna B. Barkley Scholarship. Edna was a home economics major when she was at Mountain College, and after making it big in the jam and jelly business, she created a scholarship especially for Mountain College freshmen who plan to major in home economics. The catch, however, is that candidates for the scholarship must have had a B average in high school. Again, if your child meets the criteria, he'll receive the award.

You may wonder where colleges and universities get the funds for these awards. Although quite often they don't have the cash, they waive certain financial charges for award recipients. Many colleges consider it a good investment in the long run to have a few top scholarship students strolling around campus. They please the faculty and may attract others like themselves. Moreover, if award recipients become successful at whatever they decide to do, they might someday lend their alma mater help by creating a scholarship or fund, as did our fictional Edna Barkley.

Institutional Creative Financing Plans

As an alternative approach to help the many middle-income families with college-bound children that are unable to establish need for federal or state aid, a small number of colleges and universities are coming to the rescue by offering their own creative financing plans.

The University of Pennsylvania, for example, has set up a separate office to administer the Penn Plan, which has six different options, including prepayment of four years' tuition. According to D. L. Wormley, assistant director of the Penn Plan, the program's loan options during the 1984-85 school year attracted 1,187 participants, who received a total of $17 million in loans.

"We work mainly with students who don't get aid through conventional programs," says Wormley. "The Penn Plan also assists families who may have a cash flow problem and would like to pay tuition on a monthly basis. We don't want them to be forced into choosing other schools because of money problems." Among the schools operating their own financing programs are Brandeis, Dartmouth, Duke, Harvard-Radcliffe, Haverford, Mount Holyoke, Princeton, the University of Southern California, Washington University, and Yale. Inquire about creative financing programs at the institutions your son or daughter is considering.

Appealing A Decision

What if a college has little or no aid to offer you? What if the aid administrator has explored every angle and informs you that your family is ineligible for any aid, despite your conviction that your child does indeed need some assistance? What can you do? If this happens, you contact the aid office to inquire about how your case was evaluated and determine whether any other kind of help is available.

Don't fail to inquire because you feel that it may not be cricket to disagree with what a financial aid office has offered your child. There may have been an error, or perhaps your family looks financially better off on paper that it actually is. In any event, arguing for more assistance is definitely worth a try. Besides, you may find out about other measures that are available to help you finance the expenses, such as installment payment or parent loan plans.

State-Sponsored Aid

Investigating state-sponsored programs can also turn up some needed assistance. In many parts of the country, you can apply for state-sponsored aid simply by checking a box on the FFS or the FAF. If that isn't the case where you live, you'll need a state-specific form, available from the high school guidance office. State programs offer many types of aid, such as:

▶ *competitive scholarships,* awarded on the basis of academic ability and need.

▶ *grants,* offered to needy students planning to attend public or private institutions.

▶ *tuition equalization,* which provides need-based grants to students attending in-state private colleges, to help offset the difference in cost between a public and a private education.

▶ *educational opportunity programs,* which are designed to identify, encourage, and, in some cases, subsidize students

residing in the state who are economically disadvantaged
or underprepared for postsecondary education.

▶ *work programs,* available to eligible students who want
to contribute toward their education by earning money.

To learn more about state-sponsored aid programs in your area,
contact the regional office of the U.S. Department of Education
and get the phone number of the financial aid agency in your
state. Current addresses are given below.

Region I

Connecticut	Office of Student Financial Assistance
Maine	U.S. Department of Education
Massachusetts	J. W. McCormack Post Office and
New Hampshire	Court House, Room 510
Rhode Island	Boston, MA 02109
Vermont	(617) 223-9333
New Jersey	Office of Student Financial Assistance
New York	U.S. Department of Education
Puerto Rico	26 Federal Plaza
Virgin Islands	New York, NY 10278
Panama Canal	(212) 264-4426
Zone	

Region III

Delaware	Office of Student Financial Assistance
District of	U.S. Department of Education
Columbia	P.O. Box 13716 (3535 Market Street)
Maryland	Philadelphia, PA 19101
Pennsylvania	(215) 596-0247
Virginia	
West Virginia	

Region IV

Alabama	Office of Student Financial Assistance
Florida	U.S. Department of Education
Georgia	101 Marietta Tower, Room 2203
Kentucky	Atlanta, GA 30323
Mississippi	(404) 321-4171
North Carolina	
South Carolina	

Region V

Illinois	Office of Student Financial Assistance
Indiana	U.S. Department of Education
Michigan	401 South State Street, Room 700 D
Minnesota	Chicago, IL 60605
Ohio	(312) 353-8103
Wisconsin	

Region VI

Arkansas	Office of Student Financial Assistance
Louisiana	U.S. Department of Education
New Mexico	1200 Main Tower Building, Room 2150
Oklahoma	Dallas, TX 75202
Texas	(214) 767-3811

Region VII

Iowa	Office of Student Financial Assistance
Kansas	U.S. Department of Education
Missouri	P.O. Box 901381
Nebraska	Kansas City, MO 64190-1381
	(816) 891-8055

Region VIII

Colorado	Office of Student Financial Assistance
Montana	U.S. Department of Education
North Dakota	1961 Stout Street—3rd Floor—FOB
South Dakota	Denver, CO 80294
Utah	(303) 844-3676
Wyoming	

Region IX

Arizona	Office of Student Financial Assistance
California	U.S. Department of Education
Hawaii	50 United Nations Plaza
Nevada	San Francisco, CA 94102
American Samoa	(415) 556-8382
Guam	
Trust Territory	
of the Pacific	
Islands	
Wake Island	

Region X

Alaska   Office of Student Financial Assistance
Idaho   U.S. Department of Education
Oregon   Third and Broad Building, Room 100
Washington   2901 Third Avenue
                      Seattle, WA 98121
                      (206) 442-0434

Private Aid Sources

Since it's to your benefit to consider every possible resource, let's now look at private sources of aid. A popular notion is that millions of dollars in private aid go unclaimed each year because no students or parents applied for it. On hearing this repeated at a national conference, one financial aid administrator remarked, "If you believe *that* you probably also believe in the tooth fairy." The truth is, there are no unrecorded stashes of money waiting to be claimed by needy students. Sources of aid have been exhaustively cataloged and computerized; after all, the idea is to give the money away, not to keep it a secret.

In fact, a minor industry has sprung up in recent years that offers computerized financial aid searches to families for a fee, usually about $50. But unless you have no other recourse, save your money—many high schools now have software programs that conduct similar searches for free. The way a computerized search is conducted is this: Your child fills out a brief information sheet about herself, identifying her religion, ethnic or racial background, membership in any clubs, and even her hobbies and interests. This criteria is then keyed into the computer, and sources of aid for which she is eligible are targeted. A printout of these sources normally includes an encapsulated description of the eligibility requirements, the amount of the award, the deadline for applying, and the address of the organization offering the award.

In short, there is probably more justification for believing in the tooth fairy than in the stories of millions of dollars in unclaimed educational aid—sources of financial aid are eager to make the money available.

Most private aid comes from community organizations, foundations, churches, corporations, and unions. In addition to the published sources of aid listed earlier in this chapter, check with your child's guidance counselor for leads. Some high schools provide lists of local sources of private aid. Next, contact your local

Chamber of Commerce and ask whether any community groups, such as Rotary or other civic/fraternal organizations, offer scholarships or grants to deserving young people. Then inquire at your church or at private organizations to which you belong, such as the Knights of Columbus, Elks, Moose, or the Veterans of Foreign Wars. And don't overlook your place of employment: a number of corporations offer scholarships to children of employees. Inquire at the personnel office.

As you uncover sources of aid, ask your child to create a scholarship checklist file. She should make a note card as illustrated below, and fill it in.

Have your son or daughter take the lead in contacting the chair person or a member of the selection committee for each award. Get your child involved at the outset, while you stay in the background. Private aid almost always puts the focus on the individual student, not on his parents.

When your child reaches one of the people in charge of administering the money, he should (1) make an appointment (if the source is local) and (2) during the appointment or over the phone, ask for advice on the best way to apply for the award. Not surprisingly, many private aid administrators are eager to offer advice because they would prefer to give the money away to highly motivated, as well as qualified, applicants. Your child might receive some tips too, such as "Be sure to write the strongest essay you can. We consider it a plus if you do outside research on the topic." Then have your child add this inside information to his award note cards.

After your child receives the application, he should read the instructions carefully, noting the deadline for submission, and then write a rough draft on a photocopy of the application. When the information on the entire sample application is accurate and persuasive, and has been checked for grammar and correct spelling, he should type the final version on the original, proofread it, keep a copy for his records, and send it off in the mail.

Occasionally, finalists for a scholarship or grant will be invited for an interview. Your child should approach this opportunity as she would a job interview. That is, she should be punctual, conservatively dressed, and prepared to answer exactly why she should receive the award. For additional preparation, I recommend that she bone up on current events by reading a few back issues of *Time* or *Newsweek, Vital Speeches,* and any other periodicals that stress global issues. Interviewers of

▶ Scholarship Checklist File

Name of scholarship or award: _____

Address: _____

Contact person: _____ Phone number: _____

Deadline: _____

Special requirements: ACT score ( )   SAT score ( )   Essay ( )

Interview ( )   Transcript ( )   Grade-point average ( )

Other requirements: _____

_____

scholarship candidates have a predilection for probing young people's awareness of world events. They tend to regard global curiosity as an indicator of academic success, which is not an unreasonable assumption. Finally, your teenager should definitely do some research on the scholarship itself or the awarding foundation, in case someone asks, "Do you know anything about the person who created this scholarship you're competing for?"

Whatever the outcome of the competition, your child should give the same award a try the following year. Perseverance pays off and your child might be rewarded for her pluck.

While you and your college-bound teenager are thoroughly researching all the possibilities for obtaining financial aid, common sense would suggest that you also think about what to do in case your child doesn't get any financial aid after you both have done your best. What then? There's one more opportunity I haven't mentioned: a bid for a Reserve Officer Training Corps (ROTC) scholarship.

ROTC Scholarships

College students awarded a competitive scholarship through the ROTC receive awards that cover the cost of their education, paid for by the federal government. The actual dollar value of such scholarships varies from campus to campus, but the amount covers tuition, lab fees, textbooks, and other educational expenses, plus a monthly stipend for each year the scholarship is in effect. Even nonscholarship students— those who merely enroll in the program—receive a monthly allowance during their last two years of college. Upon graduation from college, ROTC students receive a commission in the Armed Services and are expected to go on active duty for several years.

The scholarships are awarded on the basis of academic performance in high school, ACT or SAT scores, the results of a medical examination, and a personal interview. Attention is also paid to leadership potential, which can be demonstrated by athletic activities and participation in clubs and other school activities.

Not all campuses offer ROTC programs, so your child should check the catalogs of the schools he's applying to or contact a local recruiter for any of the Armed Services. A recruiter can also tell your child about reserve programs, which involve serving part-time in the military. Benefits include a steady, monthly income, eligibility for a generous enlistment bonus, and educational assistance through student loans.

Cutting College Expenses

Whether or not your child receives any outside assistance toward her education at college, there are several things that can be done to make college costs more affordable:

▶ find out whether the college offers a deferred payment plan and use that option if you anticipate difficulty paying for an entire semester at one time.

▶ take advantage of "super-saver" fares or special fare plans for all trips to and from college.

▶ buy wash-and-wear clothes to cut down on dry-cleaning expenses.

▶ keep long-distance phone calls to a minimum, or take advantage of a long-distance service such as Sprint or MCI.

▶ buy used text books at the student bookstore, instead of new ones.

▶ keep the costs of college materials as low as possible by watching student bulletin boards for offers of trades or cut prices on items such as drafting supplies, computer accessories, lab science tools, etc.

▶ take correspondence courses that award credit that can be transferred to her college.

When you think about it, lining up financial aid and budgeting money for college expenses requires the same type of effort and initiative as do other major events in life, such as buying a home, weighing job offers, or deciding to change careers. Determination and resourcefulness can really pay off (and *payoff* is exactly what you're hoping for in connection with financial aid). Look at it this way: financial aid is meant to be shared among hundreds of thousands of people every year; make up your mind that your child is going to be among the happy recipients. Give the process of applying for aid your best shot. One thing's clear, anyway: the fact that you read this lengthy chapter shows that you're certainly no quitter.

CHAPTER 12

Getting Accepted
and Accepting Denial

E ver hear of "Bloody Monday"? "Bloody Monday" is the day in mid-April when Ivy League schools notify applicants whether they've been accepted or not. As nicknames go, it might seem a little exaggerated, until you put yourself in the shoes of a college applicant.

Young people tend to read a great deal of significance into an admission committee's decision. Usually they interpret it as some indication of who will succeed in life and who won't. And let's not pull any punches: many parents pin their hopes on the outcome, too. Once I heard of a father who made sure all his friends and associates at the country club knew which prestigious schools his daughter had applied to. When in the end she was admitted to none of them, the girl's father cancelled his club membership, too ashamed to go back anymore.

You might not think your child is risking as much, but he believes he is. He wants to come through for you. He wants you to be proud of him. Even beyond pleasing the family, he probably looks forward to letters of acceptance as proof that his qualities are appreciated by society at large. Though admissions people don't use the term, a letter of denial from a college is called a "rejection" by students, which captures their interpretation perfectly. With so much hanging in the balance, is it any wonder that the period spent waiting for replies from colleges can be so nervewracking for young people?

In the meantime, what you can do is keep in mind that your child's chances of acceptance are good. From the start, students tend to choose institutions that will accept them. As one study already cited revealed, 92 percent are admitted to their first or second choice. Even so, you may find your optimism wearing thin as your child brings home daily reports about who among his friends has heard from colleges. But keep a stiff upper lip: friends' results have no bearing on your child's applications. Colleges use different methods for notifying candidates —trying to second guess the system is useless. If your child suspects that something has gone wrong, he can phone the admissions office and check on the status of his application. Feeling anxious is understandable, and admissions people won't think they're being pressured.

Responding to Offers of Admission

But finally a letter will arrive (Is the envelope thick or thin? is everyone's first question), and your child will read that on behalf of the students and faculty, the director of admissions congratulates him on being admitted as a freshman. Within a couple of weeks, the college's financial aid office will inform him of its decision too, and at last the waiting is over.

Well, not quite. In fact, under no circumstances should your child make a commitment too soon. He may be tempted to declare victory, and the college might hint that the sooner he sends in his housing deposit the better, but it's essential that he wait until all his choices reply. The reason is this: differences in financial aid offers will influence which college your child finally chooses. And until he can compare offers, the smart thing to do is to sit tight. Remember, the National Association of College Admission Counselors says in its Statement of Principles of Good Practice that students have the *right* to wait until all their choices have replied, or until May 1, whichever is earlier, so he needn't worry that he'll be left high and dry—he won't be.

Double-Depositing

Nevertheless, some students and their parents, while waiting for financial aid letters, attempt to cover their bets by sending away two or more housing deposits or other sums of money supposedly indicating the child's intent to attend. They realize they will forfeit one or more of the deposits eventually, but they evidently consider this a calculated risk. For two reasons, however, "double-depositing," as it's called, is wrong.

First, double-depositing makes things tough on admissions offices and other applicants. Once a deposit has been received, colleges take students at their word and hold a spot for them in the freshman class. Fellow applicants placed on the waiting list will eventually drop off, not realizing that some students in the accepted group won't be coming after all, despite having sent a deposit.

Second, besides the way the duplicity of double-depositing affects others, it's untrustworthy and parents who allow it are setting a poor example for their children. Choosing a college marks an important developmental milestone in a young person's life. Encouraging an act that wouldn't be tolerated even in the most competitive areas of the business world establishes a precedent of wrongdoing. And when an adult's word is no longer any good, the cornerstone of her reputation begins to crumble.

Because double-depositing has become a problem, colleges are taking action. Many will cross-check with one another by trading lists of students who have sent in a deposit. In Pennsylvania, 13 colleges have agreed to respond to discoveries of double-depositing this way: the two institutions being duped will *both* send a letter to the sly applicant saying, "We understand that you have sent a deposit to (the other school). Best wishes to you." Other colleges make it clear that they will have nothing to do with students who play tricks.

The Waiting List Dilemma

But what if your child is one of those on a waiting list—what can he do to protect himself from the impact of double-depositing by others? Waiting lists are created out of necessity and not because colleges enjoy stringing young people along. Selective colleges are forced to estimate that one-third to one-half of the students they offer admission to won't come, simply because able students are always being courted somewhere else, too. Even an institution the caliber of Harvard-Radcliffe saw one in four of the admitted freshmen for the class of 1988 enroll elsewhere. But as soon as the class begins falling below its targeted size, admissions offices go to the waiting list. Acceptance can even come in late summer. The colleges where your child has been wait-listed will keep her informed of her status, though it wouldn't hurt for her to call regularly either, especially if she's in a deadline bind because of delayed financial aid decisions from other colleges. In any case, your child can help other students by notifying all the institutions on her list as soon as she's made a final decision.

Making a Choice Among Colleges

Of course, sometimes deciding which college to attend isn't easy, and multiple acceptances compound the problem. In my talks with students, I find that many of them are struggling to figure out which would be the "perfect" college for them. But there is no perfect college, I have to say. Deciding which institution to attend, just like choosing which ones to apply to, is a matter of weighing advantages and disadvantages. The best way to reach a decision is to:

▶ define the decision to be made.

▶ recognize what's important.

▶ assess the costs and benefits.

▶ make a decision and carry through.

In a situation involving multiple acceptances, I recommend to students that they use a decision grid. Across the top should be the names of schools offering admission. And along one side, these aspects: quality of the program, cost, location, size, social climate, and physical surroundings.

Then I tell students to rate the colleges in each category 1 to 5, with 5 as the highest, and total the columns. The college with the most points is the best choice. Parents should refrain from trying to argue otherwise; ultimately, it will be the child's responsibility to adjust to the demands of college, so he must be the one to choose.

When your child has chosen a college, he or she will mail in a housing deposit. At this point your child will have taken a big step toward actually enrolling in college. But what about those colleges that denied him admission? As a parent, what should you say or not say about them? And how should you and your child deal with denial?

Dealing with Denial of Admission

Young people tend to personalize denials. Often they will read motives into the decision, such as "They're trying to say I don't have what it takes," or "This is their way of saying, 'Be realistic, kid, and quit dreaming.'" Consequently, it's important that you not let your son or daughter generalize about what the decision means. What it means in most cases is simply that the college had more qualified applicants than it had the space and staff to accommodate, a situation that occurs at a number of colleges every year.

Appealing the Denial

No admissions person would argue that the system is perfect, either. Colleges cannot know from an essay, a transcript, and a few recommendations the full circumstances of a young person's life. The system rewards applicants who have not known excessive internal conflict and those who fit the profiles the institution is looking for. If your child disagrees with the decision, she should phone the admissions office and ask for reasons, though she has to bear in mind that what's at issue is a professional judgment, and not a situation for which there is a satisfyingly exact answer. About one-quarter of colleges and universities have appeals procedures, though fewer than half routinely inform applicants that they exist. In general, private schools are more likely than public to review an application on request.

Transferring to the First Choice Junior Year

Another option your son or daughter may want to consider is transferring to his first-choice college from a two-year institution. Transfer students who were not admitted to their first choice during high school are surprised to find that a semester or more at a two-year college makes them even more attractive to four-year colleges than they were before.

"Here's what goes through the mind of a transfer student," said Rob Yacubian, Coordinator of Transfers at Greenfield Community College in Greenfield, Massachusetts. "He thinks, I'll apply to a four-year public college—that's all I'm good for. That's all I can afford. But when that student comes to see me in that frame of mind, the first thing I do is catch him off guard with, 'Have you thought about a more competitive school?' "

Yacubian's job is to encourage transfer students to think about possibilities. Too often, he finds, they want to "move over" to a four-year college that's on exactly the same level.

"They underestimate themselves, yes. But what they don't realize is that very often four-year colleges don't even look at high school grades. Community college grades count more. What admissions people realize about community college students is that maybe they weren't as mature in high school. Or maybe they just didn't get encouraged to do well in class. But that was then, this is now."

In her role as an admissions representative for the University of Pennsylvania, Kelly Higashi has read many applications from community college transfer students.

"We don't weigh the high school transcript as heavily as the one from the community college," she said. "We look at that first and foremost. It eclipses even the scores from the ACT or SAT taken in high school. The interview is very important, too."

Higashi says one of the key considerations is whether the transfer applicant has taken challenging courses at the community college.

"They don't need to retake the ACT or SAT," she said. "We just want to see the kinds of courses taken and the grades received. Usually the cutoff is a 3.0 or B average."

Overall, Yacubian said, the competitive four-year college will want to know:

▶ What has the applicant done after high school?

▶ What has she done in liberal arts courses?

▶ What kind of recommendations can he supply?

▶ Is she equal to the work?

"Very often," said Higashi, "the transfer student is a late bloomer. But he or she can definitely change the whole academic picture between high school and a four-year college."

The only word of caution I would offer has to do with using a *four-year college* as springboard to another college. This is also a plan that can work, but a student spending a year someplace where he or she doesn't really want to be runs a higher risk of attitudinal problems. Not much effort may be put into forming friendships because they might not last, and occasionally the effects of feeling impermanent or restless begin to show up in coursework, too. The final irony, then, may be that the student who always planned to transfer finds that he had better stay put and get his grades up. For these reasons, it's a better idea to attend a two-year college where most people are there for the purpose of transferring as a means of finally being admitted to that first-choice four-year institution.

Whether your child attends a two-year or four-year institution, a housing decision will be the first hurdle in establishing a relationship with his or her college of choice.

CHAPTER 13

Dorms, Co-ops, and Frats: Arranging for Housing

W hen thinking about housing at college, uppermost in your child's mind (and in yours, too) should be cost, convenience, transportation, and safety.

Generally, your child will have a choice between two kinds of student housing available, on-campus and off-campus. On-campus housing conforms to rules and regulations set by the college, although students usually can choose from various meal plans and types of accommodations. Single-sex dormitories are available on some campuses, and there are often special interest floors, where all the residents might be foreign language or computer science majors, for instance. Off-campus housing, on the other hand, can be privately or university owned.

▶ Making a Housing Choice

Residence Hall Living

Let's look at dormitories first, where most students choose to spend freshman year. From a cost standpoint, they are quite often the best deal in town. College administrators prefer that undergraduates live in dormitories for two reasons: first, dormitories are designed and constructed with students' safety in mind, and second, studies have shown that students who live in dormitories are less likely to drop out than those living on their own off campus. Hence, colleges deliberately keep the cost of living in a dormitory competitive with any other kind of arrangement, with the possible exception of living at home. From the angles of convenience and transportation, undergraduate dormitories are almost always located within walking distance of campus, or are at least connected to campus via bikepaths or bus routes, making the cost and hassle of owning a car unnecessary. As a parent concerned with your child's living conditions, you can probably appreciate that when a student lives in a dormitory, it's somebody else's responsibility to keep the lights on, the heat going, and the premises clean.

A recent trend is to regard dormitories as more than just places to eat and sleep. Housing administrators are trying to make the students' quarters an environment that will have positive influences on their total development. Honors programs have been integrated with living arrangements, for example, so that students can attend seminars or study sessions right on their own floor. Many dormitories now boast on-line terminals for students, darkrooms, videotape and motion picture rooms, and exercise equipment. This is a far cry from the days, still in recent memory, when the kid on the floor who had a plant in his room was a suspicious character.

But in spite of the improvements, two major drawbacks of dormitory life continue to be excessive noise and nonsense. While reading a student newspaper not long ago, I saw a photograph of hundreds of tiny, water-filled paper cups that had been set in perfect order from one end of a dormitory hall to the other. According to the caption, the perpetrators of the gag had stayed up all night filling and arranging the cups to prevent people from leaving their rooms. And so to class . . .

Housing Cooperatives

Another kind of on-campus living arrangement that comes close to dormitories in terms of cost, convenience, and safety is the cooperative. Residents of co-ops share the costs of maintaining the building, including the expense of having meals prepared for them. Usually living on the premises is a person acting as a supervisor with a title like the housemother, manager, or director. Cooperatives are sometimes organized around interesting themes, founded on the preferences of the residents—all might be vegetarians, for instance, or members of a particular faith.

Fraternities and Sororities

By far, fraternities and sororities are the most widely known type of on-campus private living, having returned to popularity during just the last five years. Generally referred to as the "Greek system" because of the letters used to designate individual chapters, membership in fraternities and sororities is by nomination only. As with most clubs, they are founded to promote ideals and advantages: academics through group support, competitive incentives, and scholarships and grants; social and leadership skills through officer responsibilities; committee projects and campus involvement; friendship; and moral development encouraged by peer pressure, philanthropy, and rituals that reinforce traditional behavior.

A long-term advantage of like-minded individuals living together in fraternities or sororities is that being a "Greek" may prove beneficial in later life. During a job hunt, networking may be easier if house members, past and present, refer one another to potential employers. Also, entry into some social circles is easier for someone who has been a Greek or who has belonged to a particular house.

But the feeling of belonging that comes with joining a sorority or fraternity is not without its possible cost. Sometimes being a Greek is literally more expensive. Houses usually entertain regularly, an expense shared by the members. In addition, chapter dues and other incrementals can add up.

Also, despite attempts by college policymakers, many houses continue to practice hazing or indoctrination. *The Chronicle of Higher Education,* a weekly newspaper, carries accounts of extreme indoctrination ceremonies by certain houses. And even Greeks would say that as a result of the way houses socialize mainly with other houses, friendships outside the system are usually few.

Joining the Greek system is a matter of personal choice, and your child can have an opportunity to see what fraternities or sororities offer during rush week.

Rush is usually held during the first few weeks of school, although some campuses also have a midyear rush. In a nutshell, it's as if each chapter were having an open house. Following a general orientation, groups of students visit the various houses, while the members scout for potential recruits or "pledges," as they're called. This is also the time when students thinking of pledging should be asking questions, such as:

▶ Is the organization local or national?

▶ Are scholarships available?

▶ Is there hazing? What kind?

▶ How important are academics?

▶ What will it cost to join?

Houses will invite students to return when there seems to be mutual interest, possibly for dinner or a social event. Interviews during this second round of introductions can be formal or informal. The membership will seek to get only a general impression of the potential pledges, or each guest will be asked to meet with a handful of members for a separate interview.

Houses then make "bids" on prospects they want as members, and students choose which chapter to pledge. At this point, you might be pulling for your old house—hoping your child will choose that one. But once again, a child's self-direction should be encouraged if she's to become an independent adult.

On the other side of the coin, rejection by a house is painful for some young people, who might also interpret it as an indication of unsuitability for social success. Assure your child that there is no link between the two, and that being turned down is a disappointment all future professionals occasionally encounter as they build their careers.

Independent Off-Campus Housing

Compared with all the types of living arrangements described so far, the one offering the fewest advantages for a student, apart from the opportunity to "try his wings," is independent, off-campus housing. Certainly the rent may be cheaper than alternatives, and the food will probably be cheaper (most students aren't born dieticians), and there's the chance to practice being independent, but the disadvantages are many.

First, there are always unforeseen expenses: cookware, tools, cleaning materials, furniture, paint, light bulbs, etc. Then a few repairs are often needed, which the previous tenant neglected. And a major expense can result when a roommate flunks out, transfers, or moves, sticking the remaining person with the rent.

Second, safety problems are not unknown when students live by themselves. Thieves and prowlers prefer the kinds of neighborhoods where off-campus students tend to congregate, to the well-lit and supervised blocks of college-run housing. Sometimes safety problems—broken intercoms, locks, and elevators—are the fault of landlords who, citing financial reasons, tend to treat the concerns of transient renters rather casually.

In fact, landlord problems tend to be the curse of college campuses. Student newspapers rage about predatory tactics practiced by absentee landlords who couldn't seem to care less about some dump of a building they own far away. But in fairness to landlords, they get tired of hearing hard-luck stories from students behind in the rent. Moreover, the elected officials and permanent residents in college towns tend to sympathize with the landlords. Student renters expect tax-supported services, despite the way some vandalize or misuse property, which eventually becomes a drag on real estate values. Students quickly learn to go to college-supported legal services when they have a gripe about landlords, because village boards and town councils will usually turn a deaf ear.

If all this isn't enough, off-campus students must also contend with transportation. Students are frequently compelled to find independent housing that is far from campus, and thus a car comes into the picture, with all the attendant difficulties of parking tickets, vandalism, and mechanical problems. On the whole, off-campus housing involves a lifestyle that most students would never agree to if their parents had suggested it first.

Reserving Housing Early

Whichever kind of living arrangement you and your child are comfortable with, send in a housing deposit or line up an apartment as quickly as possible. College towns are almost always tight on space, as illustrated by a recent case involving several freshmen who had been housed in a dormitory lounge for six weeks while the college tried to find them rooms. The students sued, arguing that their constitutional rights as taxpayers had been violated while they attended a state-supported university. The court responded that the college only had to guarantee them housing, not any particular kind of housing.

By mailing in a housing deposit, your child has taken a big step toward actually enrolling in college. Now that he's over the biggest hurdles of gaining acceptance and making arrangements for housing and is on his way toward graduation from high school, have you started noticing any of the behavior described in the next chapter?

CHAPTER 14

Helping Your Child
with Separation Anxiety

A high school senior with a first-semester A average in physics suddenly stops handing in his homework. A classmate, an outgoing girl, starts avoiding all her closest friends. And one clear spring night, the vice president of the student council, also about to graduate, spends an hour soaping the school windows.

What's going on?

Some call it "senior slump" or "end-of-term blues," but to school counselors and social workers this kind of behavior generally comes under the heading of "separation anxiety." And usually this collection of anxious feelings hits college-bound students hard.

It will probably seem ironic to you that after all your advice and encouragement, your child suddenly puts on the brakes at this point. But this kind of behavior is as normal for a high school student as dreading dark rooms is for a preschooler. As a parent, you can help your child resolve problems related to separation anxiety by learning to understand its sources, recognize its symptoms, and understand how your behavior will affect your child's success at clearing this final hurdle between adolescence and adulthood.

▶ Separation Anxiety

Sources and Symptoms of Separation Anxiety

Let's start by stepping back for a moment and trying to see the end of high school from the viewpoint of many college-bound students.

"As their senior year comes to an end," explains Dr. Anthony Moriarty, Director of Pupil and Personnel Services at Rich East High School in Park Forest, IL, "the general anxiety that most adolescents feel suddenly assumes a greater degree of reality.

"A major dilemma arises from the realization that, 'I spent years complaining about the system and soon, there'll be nothing to complain about.' Generally, kids don't deal up-front with these feelings, getting into 'hell raising' instead. Some kids actually sabotage their graduation—sort of snatching defeat from the jaws of victory."

Keep in mind that college represents a critical turning point in a young person's life. Up ahead looms adulthood, holding out promises of greater freedom, but also imposing new responsibilities. As some students think about this, they feel the past and the future pulling them in opposite directions. On the one hand, they experience a normal desire for more independence; on the other, they feel anxious about giving up security and dependence.

A teacher friend of mine says she notices a distinctive kind of behavior—characterized by doubt and uncertainty about the future—among her students as graduation approaches.

"The honors students," she says, "put on the brakes first. Many have just received college acceptances and are worried about what's in store for them. The second group, most of them college bound as well, begin feeling anxious about leaving home."

At New Trier High School in Winnetka, IL, Ben Wheatley, the former Chairman of Social Work Services, held intervention seminars in the homerooms of seniors. Wheatley, now in private practice, first asked students to write down their biggest concerns.

"The list," he says, "was always the same: Am I going to graduate? Will I get into the college of my choice? Will I be able to leave my friends and family comfortably?" To Wheatley, these are normal concerns that arise from having to "say good-bye to childhood."

Coping Behaviors and Strategies

To cope with the feelings that arise during this transition period, explains Wheatley, "Students must understand that separation is an ongoing process in life. Some kids would come to me and say, 'My friends and I have such deep important talks over the weekend. Then Monday comes and everyone acts so cool and distant.' What's happening is that friends are beginning to practice distancing themselves, to lessen the strain of saying good-bye."

Dealing with separation anxiety by "detachment," as Dr. Moriarty describes it, can even extend to the way students handle breaking away from school itself. Like the student who soaped the windows, some seniors become critical and condescending toward the institution that has played such a big part in their lives.

"After all," says Wheatley, "believing that the school is 'no damn good anyway' makes it a lot easier to leave."

Other examples of behaviors designed to break the ties to high school include uncharacteristic incidents of plagiarism, smoking, cutting class, or failing to turn in class assignments. Some seniors spend the first semester worrying about grades, and then during the second semester they let their standards collapse because, they say, high school is "irrelevant."

Still other students try leaping headlong into adulthood, becoming deeply involved, for instance, in romantic relationships in which both young people take on attitudes of a married couple. Occasionally these romances or friendships are with people whose values are meant to startle parents, as though the student were saying, "See, I'm competent to get along with *all* kinds of people."

While these are very noticeable types of behavior, some students aren't so direct. For instance, parents may notice their child acting bored, tired or depressed. He may complain of difficulty sleeping, or of having no appetite. On the other hand, he may start eating a lot and gain more weight in two months than he has in two years.

Changes for Parents

The tendency of most caring parents is to rush in and help any way they can. But stop a minute and recognize that this may be a rough time of life for you, as well.

About the time students are preparing for college, their parents are approaching midlife. The family is beginning to disperse. As the children go off on their own, there's a renewed focus on the marriage partnership. Mom and Dad become reacquainted with an earlier identity: that of husband and wife. Some couples relish the free time and the opportunities to set new goals. Others are thrown off balance, because they can no longer organize their lives around their children.

Think also of the financial aspects of these changes. College expenses loom just about the time parents are looking forward to enjoying the benefits derived from making earlier sacrifices. Perhaps a new (smaller) house or an opportunity for self-employment beckons. Yet when tuition bills start crowding in, parents may be forced to put aside their plans for a long time.

As a way of defining your feelings about your child leaving for college, try to answer the following questions as honestly as you can:

▶ Will your child's leaving feel like a loss to you?

▶ If your child's absence will create an empty nest, what are you planning for yourself?

▶ If you're married, do you think your marriage will be affected by these changes?

▶ How will you feel about not being able to protect your child?

▶ What expectations do you have for your child with regard to career plans, grades, etc.?

▶ When your child returns home for a visit, will you expect the former amount of obedience?

▶ Do you think your child appreciates the financial commitment being made?

Helping Your Child to Adjust

Next, realize that the "task of emancipation," as Dr. Moriarty calls it, must be shared. In other words, letting go is an adjustment you, as well as your child, must make. Try to feel and act confident about the coming changes. If you express doubt and trepidation about the future, your child's anxiety will increase, too. Be a positive example as much as possible and convey an optimistic attitude toward the future.

On the other hand, don't push too hard. Expect foot-dragging behavior on your teenager's part as some of the following important deadlines approach: the ordering of graduation ceremony cards, correspondence with colleges regarding housing deposits, final transcripts, and similar matters. It's unlikely that your child will rush through all this paperwork, because it symbolizes a decision to plunge into the unknown.

Speaking of pushing too hard, avoid making premature changes in your child's physical surroundings. You may be tempted to begin remodeling her room so that a sibling can move in eventually, but this will probably make the original owner feel like she's being pushed out the door. In my own family, dinner table jokes are still told about how I unexpectedly returned a few minutes after leaving for college, and discovered my parents and a younger brother sitting in my old room debating who should get my alarm clock. I felt like I was attending my own wake!

As a way of counteracting your child's vague, generalized apprehensions about leaving home, suggest that he keep a journal in which to analyze his feelings and ideas. A related technique is to write down a specific worry, write what can be done about it, and then decide what to do and take action. If ordinary "senioritis" — boredom, lack of interest in school and studies — is bothering him, suggest that he take a run at something entirely new. Volunteering at a hospital or working as a stagehand at the local theater company can add an exciting dimension to those last few months of high school while he is "waiting" to graduate.

In addition, your child's time would be well spent by learning to do the following, all of which are practical skills that he or she will need for self-sufficiency:

▶ How to write checks and balance a checkbook

▶ How to do laundry

▶ How to cook, using simple recipes

▶ How to clean wood furniture, windows, floors, a stove

▶ How to type or use a personal computer

▶ How to handle a charge card and pay the bills

As a way of acknowledging that it won't be long before your child is in college, you might consider making a present of the following, all of which will come in handy:

▶ A dictionary

▶ A thesaurus

▶ *The Elements of Style,* by Wilfred Strunk, Jr., and E. B. White (Macmillan, 1979).

▶ *A Manual for Writers of Term Papers, Theses and Dissertations*, by Kate S. Turabian (University of Chicago, 1973).

▶ *Writing and Researching Term Papers and Reports: A New Guide for Students,* by Eugene Ehrlich and Daniel Murphy (Bantam, 1968).

▶ A Bible

▶ *The New York Times Guide to Reference Materials,* by Mona McCormick (Times Books, 1985).

The most important thing for you and your child to remember is that separation is a necessary step in a healthy person's development. We routinely move away from things and people. Consider these experiences, all of which are common milestones in our lives: being a kindergartener and worrying about primary school; being an eighth-grader who's nervous about high school; being an adult and wondering how relocation to a new town will affect us. And everyone at some time feels sadness at parting with family members and friends.

These events spur advances in our journey to maturity. We discover that we can cope on our own and that meeting emotional challenges contributes to becoming independent. As a colleague of mine, a school psychologist, observes, "Sometimes we have to give up certain things in order to have more freedom." With your help, this outlook is one your child will come to understand. If so, it will stand your child in good stead as he or she begins the freshman year at college, which is the topic of our final chapter.

CHAPTER 15

Your Freshman at College

A s every parent knows, children do not all reach certain developmental stages at exactly the same time. All babies do not crawl at eight months; all young people do not reach puberty simultaneously; and all teenagers do not begin dating at age 16. Each of our children seems to have an inner clock that regulates when these kinds of things occur.

College students, likewise, mature at different rates. Despite enjoying many of the privileges reserved for adults—voting, securing credit, setting their own schedules, etc.—some college students have trouble finding an adult identity they're comfortable with. And the college environment itself, which encourages a search for personal truths and offers new freedoms, can push freshmen, in particular, off balance for a while. As a result, your child may experience, as do countless freshmen, a period of adjustment that is marked by self-doubt and perhaps some surprising behavior.

Testing a New Identity: Alan's Story

Consider, for example, the experiences of a young man we'll call Alan. Alan was an above-average student in high school who looked forward to being the first child in the family to attend college. As he watched the miles go by during the three-hour train trip to campus, it seemed to Alan that everything was falling into place just the way he'd hoped.

At first Alan felt a little shy as a new student, but there were plenty of "get acquainted" parties and "welcome freshmen" dances, and it wasn't long before he started making friends.

Once classes started, Alan settled into his regular study habits, but the reading assignments kept him up night after night. Then came a setback that really worried him. He handed in a five-page paper and received a D on it. Surprised, Alan made an appointment to see the instructor.

"Young man, your concern is understandable, but what I wanted was analysis," the instructor told him, "not just a summary of the lectures. Show me that you can think."

Alan did start learning how to think critically in one of the college's most popular freshman courses: Professor Middleton's Introduction to Logic and Philosophy. Middleton accepted nothing on face value. His roving intelligence attacked traditions, political events, even religion. His students would try to refute him, but he always counterattacked, starting with, "Do you really think so?" The phrase was a classic on campus, and Alan found himself using it during midnight bull sessions at the dormitory.

By the time Thanksgiving rolled around, Alan was a little sad at having to pack up and leave his new home. After his excited family met his train at the terminal, 10 minutes were spent posing for pictures, during which he acted a "little above it all," as his dad later complained to his mom.

That night, dinner was one long argument. Alan and his parents were at odds over all kinds of social issues that Alan seemed to bring up deliberately. Finally, after a long rebuttal by his dad to a statement Alan had made, Alan leaned back in his chair and said, smiling, "Do you really think so?" To which his father shot back, "Yeah, as a matter of fact I do, and I'm getting pretty sick of your attitude!" Alan's mother angrily announced she was going for a walk. Outside in the darkness, she wondered why she felt so disappointed and upset.

College hadn't ruined Alan, or his relationship with his parents. His experiences at college had merely altered his outlook, although he seemed to be flaunting the "new" Alan a bit too much. Let's step back for a moment and try to understand some of the reasons for Alan's behavior.

First, think about the high school environment he left behind. In the typical high school class, the teacher knows all the students by name and encourages them to maximize their potential. Regular parent-teacher conferences provide an opportunity for parents to talk confidentially with teachers about their child's progress. High school is a nurturing, supportive environment where young people are treated as children. Now let's sit in on a college classroom for the sake of comparison.

Here the instructor focuses on the subject to be taught and the students' understanding of it, not on the pupils themselves. As Alan discovered, merely knowing the material isn't enough; tests and assigned papers pose problem situations and challenge students to solve them. Moreover, Alan was probably puzzled by the instructor's apparent lack of sympathy about the D he received for his paper. But college-level educators aren't as concerned with grades as they are with whether their students are learning. Consequently, college students feel pulled in two directions: they compete for good grades, but their instructors emphasize learning for its own sake. To a student like Alan, who prided himself on good grades in high school, this type of teaching runs counter to his image of himself as a superior student. Some students retaliate by overcompensating. They begin posing as stereotypical intellectuals, sometimes even taking on the mannerisms and attitudes of admired instructors. Alan, for example, took Professor Middleton as his role model.

Professor Middleton is actually a rather conservative fellow, but in front of his students he plays the supreme skeptic. He won't let anyone get away with a remark he or she can't support. Alan was taken in by Middleton's act and even began imitating his opinions and his famous "Do you really think so?" But it's not unusual for college students to find role models with radical views. After all, they're trying to break away from home and establish their independence. What better way than to adopt viewpoints that are opposite to their parents'?

Naturally, by the time Alan came home for Thanksgiving, the fuse was lit. His parents had missed him and were looking forward to having him back in the fold, while he was eager to demonstrate his new powers of reasoning.

But how permanent are the changes in Alan? Will he forever be on a "higher" intellectual plane than his parents? Will he always act contemptuously toward them? Actually, most of his behavior at home and with others is superficial, part of a strategy to conceal his inner uncertainty. Young adults are trying to develop a philosophy of living. Their conversation tends to be full of evaluations of friends, family members, and social values. They insist that others be tolerant of them, while they dole out criticism.

College is a time of trial and error in sex, academics, friendships, and values. No one should graduate as exactly the same person that his or her parents sent off four years earlier. Many students experience positive mental and emotional changes and find themselves exercising greater concern for others, enjoying higher self-esteem, and moving away from self-absorption. Gradually they begin to act independently because they feel they have control over themselves.

Student Stress and Some Possible Responses to It

But these kinds of changes are not accomplished without some stress, too. Let's compare causes and symptoms of normal stress versus extreme stress.

Linda, for instance, discovered early in her freshman year that time management was her biggest problem. Her reading assignments were lengthy, but what prevented her from keeping up with her work was a handful of friends who would stop by nearly every night and stick around to talk. By midnight she was tired, too tired to do much studying. Two weeks before final exams, she had to stay up night after night, writing last-minute papers and reading dozens of chapters. When she came home for vacation, she complained that instructors heaped work on her. Too much stress? No, by second semester she resolved to limit her partying to weekends and study during the week.

Don, on the other hand, went overboard. Afraid that college was going to be too much of a challenge for him, he did nothing *except* study. Every upcoming test was a source of great anxiety; every paper he wrote went through many drafts until he despaired of ever being able to say what he wanted to say. His roommate tried to persuade him that he was setting his goals too high, but Don continued hurling himself at the books. He lost weight and became defensive over trivial issues. Fortunately, the resident advisor on his floor had been observing him. The advisor made a point of regularly inviting Don to his room for heart-to-hearts about school, grades, and other concerns. On the advisor's recommendation, Don signed up for a seminar on stress management at the student health clinic. As a result, he learned how to recognize when he was going into one of his crisis modes, and how to avoid feeling panicky about his grades.

Finally, let's look at an example of extreme stress in a girl named Eve. Almost from the moment her parents dropped her off at the dormitory, they suspected that something was wrong. Instead of acting excited, Eve was withdrawn. She called a few days later, crying and saying that everyone seemed cold and unfriendly. Subsequent calls were long and unhappy, filled with complaints of being unable to concentrate and fears that people would "discover I'm a failure." Right before final exams, Eve's roommate called and said Eve seemed depressed all the time and was sleeping through her morning classes. Her father came to campus immediately and stayed for a few days. The two of them went to a walk-in counseling clinic provided by the university, where a psychologist recommended that Eve participate in twice-weekly group sessions with other students. Although Eve finished the year on academic probation, her parents noticed that her attitude was improving. The following fall, she attended the sessions only once a week, and eventually dropped them altogether. By junior year, she had found a major she enjoyed and, in her words, was "on the home stretch."

Student ailments brought on by extreme stress include fatigue, high blood pressure, depression, and sometimes drug or alcohol abuse. Although your child will inevitably experience some rough times associated with the rigors of college, you can recognize signs of real unhappiness: your son or daughter repeatedly makes long, tearful phone calls home, or wants to come home for a visit at every opportunity, for example. Take notice too if your child seems to be losing a lot of weight, or if he's constantly complaining of illness or fatigue.

If your child seems to be under more than a normal amount of stress, you might encourage her to take advantage of university health services; most institutions maintain counseling clinics for students. On many campuses, as we saw in Eve's case, group therapy is also offered. In addition, college towns often have HELP or CRISIS lines; phone numbers for these lines are posted in cafes, laundromats, and other places that students frequent.

Ways Parents Can Help

If, on the other hand, you feel your child's difficulties are the usual ones associated with change, try to convey confidence. The following sections describe some supportive things you can do.

Show Interest

Take an interest in your child's academic and social life. Ask questions about your child's classes. Express interest in seeing some of her written assignments. One student reported being embarrassed, but was clearly pleased, that her father took one of her papers into work to show his colleagues. The same kind of pride you took in your child's accomplishments early in her academic career is still appropriate. Likewise, try to be on campus for homecoming or some other major social event so that you can appreciate your child's lifestyle outside class, too.

Listen

Listen with an open mind to talk of changing majors and other speculations about the future. College students change majors three times on the average and usually come back to their original choice. It's part of being in an environment where many different and intriguing careers beckon. One semester your child might talk of majoring in finance, then express interest in international business, then take a class in organizational psychology, which inspires him with thoughts of being an industrial psychologist . . . no, a personnel manager . . . no, a consultant on human resource development. Finding one's way is part of the process of maturing; the most constructive thing you can do is listen attentively as your child's plans evolve.

Give Encouragement and Advice

Offer advice and encouragement. Keep in mind that your child may still want to use you as a sounding board. Your reaction to her decisions and plans is important. Responding with advice and encouragement, when they would be welcome, is helpful.

Send Letters

Send letters regularly about events at home and family members, especially during freshman year. News from home helps prevent college students from feeling adrift in a place of shifting values and unfamiliar challenges. Your "care packages" of cookies and photographs will remind your child that she has a network of family members who love her.

Give Choice

Let your child accept the consequences of his own decisions. Your child may talk of dropping out for a year or switching campuses. If you're satisfied that he's researched his decision, allow your child the opportunity to test out a hunch or go in a new direction. Who knows? In retrospect, it may have been exactly the right move at the right time. With each succeeding decision your child makes independently, he will increase his ability at making new and perhaps more difficult choices.

Clashes will be inevitable as both of you try to become

accustomed to the "new order" of things. Disagreements will tend to crop up during visits home and vacations ("What do you mean 'the midnight curfew is still in force in this house'? At college, I haven't been in before midnight in months!"). And conversations that veer toward controversial topics will occasionally provoke hot responses on both sides. But by your child's sophomore year, you will begin to notice a new sense of tolerance on his or her part—maybe even a glimmer of appreciation for all you've accomplished and done.

And you have done a lot. You deserve to feel proud.

Glossary

Accreditation — Official recognition that a college, university, or trade school has met the standards of a regional or national association.

Achievement Tests — Administered in a variety of academic subjects and sometimes required by colleges for the purpose of placement in freshman courses, as well as for the admissions decision process. Students often take Achievement Tests at the end of their junior year or in the middle of their senior year.

ACT — Administered by the American College Testing Program, this test measures educational development in English, mathematics, social studies, and the natural sciences. Scores are reported as 1 to 36, with 36 as highest.

Advanced Placement (AP) Credit — An examination is administered and scored 1 to 5, with 5 as the highest. Each college or university decides how much credit, if any, it will grant the student.

Application for Federal Student Aid (FASA) — Federal form that may be used in applying for Pell Grants and federal campus-based aid.

Associate Degree — Awarded by a college or university after satisfactory completion of a two-year program of study.

Award Letter — Document issued to a student financial aid recipient that indicates the type, amount, and disbursement dates of the funds awarded for the various financial aid programs.

Baccalaureate, or Bachelor's Degree — Awarded by a college or university after satisfactory completion of a four-year program of study.

Basic Educational Opportunity Program — See Pell Grant.

Campus-based Aid—Financial assistance for students and their families administered by a college. Funds, regardless of their source, are awarded to students by the college's financial aid office and not by a state, federal, or private agency.

Candidates Reply Data Agreement (CRDA)—Allows students to defer attendance decisions at participating colleges until May 1. This enables students to hear from most of the colleges they have applied to before having to select.

College-Level Examination Program (CLEP)—Provides an opportunity for examinees to demonstrate and receive college credit for competency obtained through life experiences. The test consists of five general examinations, and several covering specific subject matter. Some colleges grant credit to students who demonstrate competency on the exam.

College Scholarship Service (CSS)—Processes the Financial Aid Form (FAF) and disseminates the information to institutions and state and federal agencies.

College Work-Study Program—Offers part-time work to eligible students who are attending classes at least half-time. This is a government-supported financial aid program administered through college financial aid offices. The work is usually college related.

Consortium—Association of two or more educational institutions that allows students to share the facilities and course offerings at member campuses. Consortiums are usually made up of neighboring colleges or universities.

Cooperative Work-Study Education—Provides full-time paid employment related to a student's field of study. The student alternates between work and full-time study. As a result, the Bachelor's program usually takes five years to complete.

Credit by Examination—Grants college credit based on the results of scores on Advanced Placement Examinations, Achievement Tests, the ACT Proficiency Examination Program (PEP), the College-Level Examination Program (CLEP), the New York College Proficiency Examination Program, the New York Regents External Degree Examination Program, or an examination specially developed by the college.

Cross-Registration—Allows students to take courses for credit at another institution without having to apply for admission.

Deferred Admission—Allows an accepted student to postpone admission for one year.

Dependent Student—A student who is dependent upon his parents or guardian for financial support or who does not meet the criteria for classification as an independent student.

Early Action—Gives special consideration to a student who applies for admission by a specified date, usually in early fall.

Early Admission—Admits students of unusually high ability into college courses and programs before they have completed high school.

Early Decision—Same as an Early Action, but if admitted, the student has an obligation not to accept an offer of admission from another institution at a later date.

Early Entrance—an opportunity to enroll in college before the senior year in high school.

Early Evaluation—A procedure adopted by the Ivy League colleges, plus MIT, in 1973. In December or January, these colleges send every applicant an evaluation of his chances of admission: Likely, Possible, and Unlikely.

Endowment—Monies invested by a college or university to produce income to help meet institutional costs.

Expected Family Contribution—Amount that parents and the student can reasonably be expected to pay for postsecondary education. For dependent students this includes the sum of the amounts that reasonably may be expected from the student (and spouse) to meet the student's cost of education and the amount that may be expected to be made available by his or her parents for this purpose.

Family Financial Statement (FFS)—Used by the American College Testing Program to analyze a family's potential contribution toward college expenses. The information is forwarded to colleges chosen by the student.

Financial Aid Form (FAF)—The College Scholarship Service's counterpart to the FFS. Some colleges prefer that applicants use the FAF, some the FFS. Many accept both. Check the back of either form to see which colleges prefer it.

Financial Aid Package—A financial aid award to a student from a combination of two or more sources of financial aid.

4-1-4 System—A semester starts in late August and ends prior to the Christmas holidays. Students then have the choice of using January as a vacation period or for special short courses lasting approximately four weeks. The second semester begins in late January or early February. Credits are reported in semester hours.

GED (Tests of General Educational Development)—Series
of five tests that students without a high school diploma
may take to qualify for a high school equivalency certificate.
Tests cover correctness and effectiveness of expression,
interpretation of reading matter in the social sciences
and natural sciences, interpretation of library materials,
and general mathematical ability. Colleges will often
accept GED results as evidence of satisfactory high school
completion.

Gift Aid—Student financial aid that does not require repayment
or require that work be performed. This includes grants and
scholarships.

Grade-Point Average (GPA)—Indicates a student's overall
scholastic performance. Is computed by assigning a point
value to each grade (for example, A = 5, B = 4, C = 3,
D = 2, F = 1), adding the total, and then dividing the total
by the number of grades.

Guaranteed Student Loan (GSL)—Made available through participating lending institutions, such as banks, savings and loan
associations, and credit unions. Repayment begins six months
after graduation.

Independent, Self-Supporting Student—Student who, during
the last calendar year or during the calendar year for which
he or she is requesting aid, has not done (and will not do) the
following: 1) be claimed as an exemption for federal income
tax purposes by his or her parents, 2) receive financial assistance of more than the amount stated on current financial aid
applications; or 3) live in the home of a parent for more than
six weeks. Exception: Students who are married at the time
they file the FAF, FFS, or AFSA need only meet the above
criteria for the calendar year for which they are requesting
aid—not the prior year.

Independent Study—Allows a student to earn credit through
self-designed coursework, which is usually planned and
evaluated by a faculty member.

Interdisciplinary—Describes programs or courses that use the
knowledge from a number of different academic fields.

Major—Area of concentration in a particular field of study.
Usually students specialize in their majors during the junior
and senior years at college.

Need Analysis Form—General term used to cover all
forms that collect information about a dependent student's

financial situation for the purpose of determining whether his or her family demonstrates financial need.

Open Admissions Policy—Allows all high school graduates to enter the college. Often, institutions with open admissions also have programs that admit students without high school diplomas.

Pell Grant—Financial aid awarded by the federal government to be used toward tuition, room and board, books, fees, and other educational expenses. This grant is provided as the foundation or "floor" of a larger financial aid package, and need not be repaid.

Pennsylvania Higher Education Assistance Agency Document—Used by Pennsylvania residents to determine eligibility for state aid. Also used in certain situations to award institutional or campus-based federal aid.

Perkins Loan Program—Federally funded, low-interest loan made available by individual colleges and based on financial need. Repayment begins six months after graduation.

Preliminary Scholastic Aptitude Test/National Merit Scholarship Qualifying Test (PSAT/NMSQT)—This shorter version of the Scholastic Aptitude Test (SAT), administered by high schools in October, assists students and their counselors in making college plans. It also serves as the qualifying exam for scholarships awarded by the National Merit Scholarship Corporation and others.

Quarter System—Divides the nine-month academic year into three equal parts of approximately 12 weeks each. Summer sessions, if any, are usually the same length. Credits are granted as quarter hours (three quarter hours = two semester hours).

Registrar—College official who registers students and collects fees. The registrar also may be responsible for keeping permanent records, maintaining student files, and forwarding copies of students' transcripts to employers and schools.

Reserve Officer Training Corps (ROTC)—Combines military education with college study leading to the baccalaureate degree. For students who commit themselves to future service in the Army, Navy, or Air Force, there is usually an offer of financial aid. Not all campuses offer ROTC.

Residency Requirements—Length of time stipulated by colleges or universities that students must spend on campus taking courses. Also refers to the period of time, set by states, that families or students must reside in the state before being considered eligible for state aid.

Rolling Admissions — An admissions procedure by which the college considers each student's application as soon as all the required credentials, such as school record and test scores, have been received. The college usually notifies applicants of its decision without delay.

Scholastic Aptitude Test (SAT) — The most widely required examination by colleges, the SAT is divided into two sections: verbal and mathematical. The Test of Standard Written English (TSWE) is administered at the same sitting. SAT scores are reported on a 200-800 scale. TSWE scores are reported on a 20-60 + scale.

Semester System — Divides the academic year into two equal segments of approximately 18 weeks each. Summer sessions are shorter, but require more intensive study.

Student Aid Application for California (SAAC) — Used by the state of California to evaluate residents applying for state aid, and processed by the College Scholarship Service. This form can also be used by California students when applying for a Pell Grant.

Student Aid Index — Numeric value reported on the Student Aid Report (SAR) that indicates the level of contribution expected by the Pell Grant program from the student/family according to the data provided by the family.

Student Aid Report — Student's official notification from the processing center of the results of his or her need analysis form. To receive payment, the student must submit the document to the financial aid office at the institution where he or she enrolls.

Student Descriptive Questionnaire (SDQ) — Questionnaire that can be completed by students when registering to take the Scholastic Aptitude Test (SAT) or an Achievement Test. The questionnaire collects information about the student's educational objectives, extracurricular interests, and goals. The information, along with the test scores, is sent to colleges and scholarship sponsors designated by the student. If the student gives permission, responses also are used by the Student Search Service, in which hundreds of colleges and universities participate.

Supplemental Educational Opportunity Grant (SEOG) — Provides assistance to students who demonstrate financial need. This is a federal program administered by colleges.

Test of English as a Foreign Language (TOEFL)—Helps foreign students demonstrate their ability to understand the English language. Many colleges require foreign students to take this test, sponsored by the College Board and the Graduate Record Examination Board, as a routine part of the application process.

3-2 Liberal Arts and Career Program—Offers a student three years of study in a liberal arts field followed by two years of professional or technical study. The student is awarded the Bachelor of Arts and the Bachelor of Science degrees upon successful completion of the program.

Transcript—Official record of a student's coursework at a school or college. A transcript is generally required as part of the college application process.

Trimester System—Divides the calendar year into three segments, thereby creating a continuous academic calendar of three semesters, each approximately 18 weeks in length. Credits are usually granted in semester hours.

50 College Summer Programs For High School Students

The American University

The American University
Summer College
The American University
4400 Massachusetts Avenue, NW
Washington, DC 20016
(202) 686-2845

Barnard College

Summer in New York
Barnard's PreCollege Program
Dean Flora Davidson
Office of Special Academic
  Programs
Barnard College-Columbia
  University
3009 Broadway
New York, NY 10027-6598
(212) 280-8866

Bennington College

Bennington July Program
Bennington College
Bennington, VT 05201
(802) 442-5401

Berklee College of Music

Summer Performance Program
Berklee College of Music
1140 Boylston Street
Boston, MA 02215
(617) 266-1400

Boston College

The Boston College Experience
Summer Session
Boston College
Chestnut Hill, MA 02167
(617) 552-3100

Brevard College

School for Gifted Students in
  the Arts
Brevard College
Brevard, NC 28712
(704) 883-8292, Ext. 212

Brown University

Summer College
Brown University
Box 1920
Providence, RI 02912
(401) 863-2785

Carnegie Mellon University

Precollege Program in the
  Fine Arts
Director of Summer Studies
Summer Studies Office
Carnegie Mellon University
5000 Forbes Avenue
Pittsburgh, PA 15213
(412) 578-6620

Central Wyoming College

Summer Session
Central Wyoming College
Riverton, WY 82501
(307) 856-9291

Connecticut College

Connecticut College Summer
　Campus
Connecticut College
New London, CT 06320
(203) 447-7566

Cornell University

Cornell University Summer
　College
Box 85
B12 Ives Hall
Ithaca, NY 14853
(607) 256-6203

Duke University

Precollege Program
01 West Duke Building
Duke University
Durham, NC 27708
(919) 684-3847

Earlham College

Explore-a-College
Summer Programs
Box 23
Earlham College
Richmond, IN 47374
(317) 962-6561

Eastern Illinois University

Spanish Summer Camp for High
　School Students
Office of Continuing Education
205 Old Main
Eastern Illinois University
Charleston, IL 61920
(217) 581-2223

Grinnell College

Office of Summer Programs
P.O. Box 805
Grinnell College
Grinnell, IA 50112-0810
(515) 236-2100

Hampshire College

Summer Studies in Mathematics
Hampshire College
Box SS
Amherst, MA 01002
(413) 549-4600, Ext. 357

Harvard University

Harvard University Secondary
　School Students Program
20 Garden Street
Harvard University
Cambridge, MA 02138
(617) 495-3192

Illinois Institute of Technology

Women in Science and
　Engineering:
Summer Program for High
　School Girls
IIT Center
Chicago, IL 60616-3793
(312) 567-3025

Illinois State University

Summer Academy
College of Continuing Education
　and Public Service
Illinois State University
Normal, IL 61761
(309) 483-8691

Indiana University

Office of Summer Sessions
Maxwell Hall, Dept. B
Indiana University
Bloomington, IN 47405
(812) 335-0661

Johns Hopkins University

Center for the Advancement of
Academically Talented Youth
The Johns Hopkins University
Baltimore, MD 21218
(301) 338-8427

Macalester College

Twin City Institute for Talented
Youth
Macalester College
1600 Grand Avenue
St. Paul, MN 55105
(612) 696-6590

Mary Baldwin College

Special Interest Summer
Programs
Mary Baldwin College
Staunton, VA 24401
(703) 885-0811 Ext. 276

Michigan Technological University

Summer Youth Program
Michigan Technological
University
Houghton, MI 49931
(906) 487-2219

Moorhead State University

Secondary School Summer
Session
Moorhead State University
Moorhead, MN 56560
(218) 236-2762

Mount Holyoke College

Summermath
302 Shattuck Hall
Mount Holyoke College
South Hadley, MA 01075
(413) 538-2608

Pacific Lutheran University

Summer Camps for High School
Students
Pacific Lutheran University
Tacoma, WA 98447
(206) 535-7453

Purdue University

Summer Engineering Seminar
Freshman Engineering
Purdue University
West Lafayette, IN 47907
(317) 494-1776

Rutgers University— Camden Campus

Rutgers Dean's Summer
Scholars Program
University College — Camden
329 Cooper Street
Camden, NJ 08102
(609) 757-6098

Saint Lawrence University

St. Lawrence University Summer
Program
Canton, NY 13617
(315) 379-5991

Saint Louis College of Pharmacy

Career Institute for High School
Juniors
St. Louis College of Pharmacy
Admissions Department
4588 Parkview Place
St. Louis, MO 63110
(314) 367-8700

Saint Xavier College

Summer Junior Program
St. Xavier College
3700 W. 103rd Street
Chicago, IL 60655
(312) 779-3300

Skidmore College

PASS
Skidmore College
Sarasota Springs, NY 12866
(518) 584-5000 Ext. 2264

Southern Methodist University

College Preparatory Institutes
Southern Methodist University
Dallas, TX 75275
(214) 692-2981

Tufts University

Focus at Tufts
P.O. Box 4
Tufts University
Medford, MA 02155
(617) 625-4850

Union College

The College Experience
Wells House
Union College
1 Union Avenue
Schenectady, NY 12308
(518) 370-6288

University of California at Berkeley

Summer Session
University of California at
  Berkeley
Berkeley, CA 94720
(415) 642-5611

University of Colorado at Boulder

Young Scholars Summer Session
Farrand Hall
Campus Box 100
University of Colorado
Boulder, CO 80310
(303) 492-6694

University of Dayton

Women in Engineering Program
School of Engineering
University of Dayton
Dayton, OH 45469-0001
(513) 229-4411

University of Illinois at Urbana-Champaign

Mathematics Camps for Gifted
  High School Students
Math Summer Programs
Conferences and Institutes
116 Illini Hall
725 S. Wright Street
University of Illinois
Champaign, IL 61820
(217) 333-2881

University of Kansas

Summer Camps and Institutes
University of Kansas
Lawrence, KS 66045
(913) 864-4422

University of Michigan

Honors Summer Institute
1210 Angell Hall
University of Michigan
Ann Arbor, MI 48109-1003
(313) 764-6272

University of Northern Colorado

Summer Enrichment Program
University of Northern Colorado
Greeley, CO 80639
(303) 351-2683

University of Notre Dame

Career Discovery Program in
  Architecture
School of Architecture
University of Notre Dame
Notre Dame, IN 46556
(219) 239-7505

University of Oregon

Summer Enrichment Program for
Talented and Gifted Students
University of Oregon
Eugene, Oregon 97403
(503) 686-5521

University of Pennsylvania

Precollege Program
University of Pennsylvania
210 Logan Hall
Philadelphia, PA 19104
(215) 898-3526

University of Wisconsin at Madison

Summer Sessions
Summer Sessions Office
University of Wisconsin
433 North Murray Street
Madison, WI 53706
(608) 262-2116

Washington and Lee University

Summer Scholars
Washington and Lee University
Lexington, VA 24450
(703) 463-8723

Washington University

Architecture Discovery Program
School of Architecture
Campus Box 1079
Washington University
St. Louis, MO 63130
(314) 889-6000

Wellesley College

Exploration Summer Program
124 High Rock Lane
Wellesley College
Westwood, MA 02090
(617) 329-4488

Phi Beta Kappa Colleges

Alabama

Birmingham-Southern
College
University of Alabama

Arizona

Arizona State University
University of Arizona

Arkansas

University of Arkansas

California

California State
University Long Beach
Claremont McKenna
College
Mills College
Occidental College
Pomona College
San Diego State
University
San Francisco State
University
Scripps College
Stanford University

University of California
Berkeley
Davis
Irvine
Los Angeles
Riverside
San Diego
Santa Barbara
Santa Cruz
University of the
Redlands
University of Santa Clara
University of Southern
California

Colorado

Colorado College
Colorado State University
University of Colorado
University of Denver

Connecticut

Connecticut College
Trinity College
University of
Connecticut
Wesleyan University
Yale University

Delaware

University of Delaware

Florida

Florida State University
Stetson University
University of Florida
University of Miami

Georgia

Agnes Scott College
Emory University
Morehouse College
University of Georgia

Idaho

University of Idaho

Illinois

Augustana College
Illinois College
Knox College
Lake Forest College
Northwestern University
Rockford College
University of Chicago
University of Illinois
    Chicago
    Urbana

Indiana

De Pauw University
Earlham College
Indiana University
Purdue University
University of Notre Dame
Wabash College

Iowa

Coe College

Cornell College
Drake University
Grinnell College
Iowa State University
Luther College
University of Iowa

Kansas

Kansas State University
University of Kansas

Kentucky

Centre College
University of Kentucky

Louisiana

Louisiana State
   University
Tulane University

Maine

Bates College
Bowdoin College
Colby College
University of Maine

Maryland

Goucher College
Johns Hopkins University
University of Maryland
Western Maryland College

Massachusetts

Amherst College
Boston College
Boston University
Brandeis University
Clark University
College of the Holy Cross
Harvard University

Massachusetts Institute
of Technology
Mount Holyoke College.
Radcliffe College
Smith College
Tufts University
University of
Massachusetts
Wellesley College
Wheaton College
Williams College

Michigan

Albion College
Alma College
Hope College
Kalamazoo College
Michigan State
University
University of Michigan
Wayne State University

Minnesota

Carleton College
College of Saint
Catherine
Hamline University
Macalester College
Saint Olaf College
University of Minnesota

Missouri

Saint Louis University
University of Missouri
Washington University

Montana

Nebraska

University of Nebraska

Nevada

New Hampshire

Dartmouth College
University of New
Hampshire

New Jersey

Drew University
Princeton University
Rutgers-The State University of New Jersey

New Mexico

University of New
Mexico

New York

City University of
New York
Brooklyn College
City College
Herbert H. Lehman
College
Hunter College
Queens College
Colgate University
Columbia University
Cornell University
Elmira College
Fordham University
Hamilton College
Hobart College
Hofstra University
Manhattan College
New York University
Saint Lawrence
University
Skidmore College

State University of
New York
Albany
Binghamton
Buffalo
Stony Brook
Syracuse University
Union College
University of Rochester
Vassar College
Wells College

North Carolina

Davidson College
Duke University
University of North
Carolina
Chapel Hill
Greensboro
Wake Forest University

North Dakota

University of North
Dakota

Ohio

Bowling Green State
University
Case Western Reserve
University
College of Wooster
Denison University
Hiram College
Kent State University
Kenyon College
Marietta College
Miami University
Oberlin College
Ohio State University
Ohio University

Ohio Wesleyan University
University of Cincinnati

Oklahoma

University of Oklahoma

Oregon

Reed College
University of Oregon

Pennsylvania

Allegheny College
Bucknell University
Chatham College
Dickinson College
Franklin and Marshall
College
Gettysburg College
Gustavus Adolphus
College
Haverford College
Lafayette College
Lehigh University
Muhlenberg College
Pennsylvania State
University
Swarthmore College
Temple University
University of
Pennsylvania
University of Pittsburgh
Villanova University
Washington and Jefferson
College
Wilson College

Rhode Island

Brown University
University of Rhode
Island

South Carolina

Furman University
University of South
   Carolina
Wofford College

South Dakota

University of South
Dakota

Tennessee

Fisk University
Rhodes College
University of the South
University of Tennessee
Vanderbilt University

Texas

Baylor University
Rice University
Southern Methodist
   University
Texas Christian
   University
Trinity University
University of Texas

Utah

University of Utah

Vermont

Middlebury College
University of Vermont

Virginia

College of William and
   Mary

Hampden-Sydney College
Mary Baldwin College
Mary Washington College
Randolph-Macon College
Randolph-Macon
   Woman's College
Sweet Briar College
University of Richmond
University of Virginia
Virginia Polytechnic Institute
   and State University
Washington and Lee
   University

Washington

University of Puget Sound
University of Washington
Washington State Uni-
   versity
Whitman College

West Virginia

West Virginia University

Wisconsin

Beloit College
Lawrence University
Marquette University
Ripon College
University of Wisconsin
   Madison

Wyoming

University of Wyoming

What to Take to College

Personal Hygiene Items

after-shave lotion
bath oil
cold cream
cosmetics
dental floss
deodorant
hair brush & comb
nail file
razor blades
shampoo
shaving cream
suntan lotion
toothbrush
toothpaste
towels

Health Items

aspirin
bandages
first-aid kit
first-aid ointment
gauze
scale
thermometer

Appliances

alarm clock
extension cord
hair dryer
iron
radio
stereo
TV

Kitchen Items

bottle opener
can opener
coffee mugs
electric pot
glasses
knives & forks
plates

Cleaning and Laundry Items

detergent
dustcloth
laundry bag
shoe polish
starch

Desk & Study Items

calculator
correction fluid
dictionary
envelopes
highlighters
notebooks
paper clips
pencils
pens
stamps
stapler
style manual

thesaurus
typewriter
typing paper

Maintenance Items

hammer
needles & thread
scissors
screwdriver
tape
thumbtacks
wrench

Index

B

C

E

Early Admission. *See* Colleges, four-year
Early Decision application, 18
Early Entrance program, 35
Educational consultant. *See* Counselor, independent
Electives. *See* Coursework, high school
Enrollment statistics, 68, 112
Essay, personal. *See* Admission process; Application process
Expenses, college, 121, 124, 143
Extracurricular involvement. *See also* Admission process;
     Application process
—college: and commuting, 39-40; described in handbooks,
     47; and size of school, 47, 59
—high school: describing on application, 102; during
     junior year, 33-34

F

Faculty. *See* Choice of college
Fairs, college: as information source, 51-53, 74; and
     minority students, 93; and recruitment mailings,
     71; timetable for, 16-17, 25
Family Financial Statement (FFS). *See* Financial aid
Family Rights and Privacy Act of 1974. *See* Buckley Amendment
Financial aid. *See also* Choice of college; National
     Achievement Scholarship Program for Outstanding Negro
     Students; National Hispanic Scholar Award Program
—acknowledgement report, 131
—applying for: advantages, 126; tips for completing
     application, 130-31; when to apply, 126, 127
—circumstances affecting award, 122-23, 127-29
—denial of, 136
—expenses, college, 121, 124
—federal aid: College Work-Study program, 133;
     Guaranteed Student Loan (GSL), 133-34; Parent Loan for
     Undergraduate Students (PLUS), 134; Pell Grant/Student
     Aid Report, 132; Perkins Loan Program, 133;
     Supplemental Educational Opportunity Grant (SEOG), 132
—forms: Family Financial Statement (FFS) and Financial Aid
     Form (FAF), 19, 126-27, 128, 129, 130, 131, 136-37;
     obtaining, 126-27; when to submit, 126, 129; who should
     file, 128-29

G

H

Other Books of Interest from the College Board

003144   *Index of Majors, 1988–89.* Lists 500 majors at the 3,000 colleges and graduate institutions, state by state, that offer them. ISBN: 0-87447-314-4, $13.95 (Updated annually)

002911   *Profiles in Achievement,* by Charles M. Holloway. Traces the careers of eight outstanding men and women who used education as the key to later success. (Hardcover, ISBN: 0-87447-291-1, $15.95); 002857 paperback (ISBN: 0-87447-285-7, $9.95)

002598   *Succeed with Math,* by Sheila Tobias. A *practical* guide that helps students overcome math anxiety and gives them the tools for mastering the subject in high school and college courses as well as the world of work. ISBN: 0-87447-259-8, $12.95

003039   *10 SATs: Third Edition.* Ten actual, recently administered SATs plus the full text of *Taking the SAT,* the College Board's official advice. ISBN: 0-87447-303-9, $9.95

002571   *Writing Your College Application Essay,* by Sarah Myers McGinty. An informative and reassuring book that helps students write distinctive application essays and explains what colleges are looking for in these essays. ISBN: 0-87447-257-1, $9.95

002474   *Your College Application,* by Scott Gelband, Catherine Kubale, and Eric Schorr. A step-by-step guide to help students do their best on college applications. ISBN: 0-87447-247-4, $9.95

To order by direct mail any books not available in your local bookstore, please specify the item number and send your request with a check made payable to the College Board for the full amount to: College Board Publications, Department M53, Box 886, New York, New York 10101-0886. Allow 30 days for delivery. An institutional purchase order is required in order to be billed, and postage will be charged on all billed orders. Telephone orders are not accepted, but information regarding any of the above titles is available by calling Publications Customer Service at (212) 713-8165.